THE U.S. OF EH?

HOW CANADA SECRETLY CONTROLS THE UNITED STATES

AND WHY THAT'S OK

By Kerry Colburn & Rob Sorensen

CHRONICLE BOOKS
SAN FRANCISCO

Library of Congress Cataloging-in-Publication Data:

Colburn, Kerry.
   The U.S. of eh? : how Canada secretly controls the United States* : *and why that's OK / by Kerry Colburn and Rob Sorensen.
      p. cm.
   ISBN 978-0-8118-6370-4
   1. Canada—Humor. 2. Canadians—United States—Humor. 3. Canadian wit and humor.
I. Sorensen, Rob. II. Title.

PN6231.C19C65 2008
818'.607—dc22

2008010664

Manufactured in CANADA.
Designed by Sara Gillingham, who is Canadian.
Photo montages created by Sara Gillingham.

10 9 8 7 6 5 4 3 2 1

Chronicle Books LLC
680 Second Street
San Francisco, California 94107
www.chroniclebooks.com

IMAGE CREDITS: P3: Beaver © Simon Phipps/istockphoto.com; p5: Goose © Noegruts/istockphoto.com; Moose © Spydr/Dreamstime.com; Beaver © Wulfespirit/Dreamstime.com; p7: Abraham Lincoln photo courtesy of Library of Congress, Prints & Photographs Division; Flag © Jocky/Dreamstime.com; p11: Mt. Rushmore © Iofoto/Dreamstime.com; Beaver © Simon Phipps/istockphoto.com; Moose © Spydr/Dreamstime.com; Geese © Alain/Dreamstime.com; p15: Igloo © Bruno Sinnah/istockphoto.com; Book © Ginosphotos/Dreamstime.com; pp24–25: Beaver © Vchphoto/Dreamstime.com; Globe © Kuzma/Dreamstime.com; Satellite © Christopher Nolan/istockphoto.com; p33: Film Reel © vndrpttn/istockphoto.com; Beaver © Steve Raubenstein/istockphoto.com; p35: Beaver © Shootalot/Dreamstime.com; Suitcase © Steve Dibblee/istockphoto.com; p36: Television © Shaun Lowe/istockphoto.com; p41: Maple Syrup © Daniel Weidemann/istockphoto.com; Syringe © Jakob Semeniuk/istockphoto.com; Beaver © Vchphoto/Dreamstime.com; p42: Hand © Howard Sandler/istockphoto.com; p46: Moose © Spydr/Dreamstime.com; Newspaper © RMackay/Dreamstime.com; p48: Curtain © Tobkatrina/Dreamstime.com; Goose © Mmphotography/Dreamstime.com; pp50–51 Film strip © David Mingay/istockphoto.com; Quebec City © Gary Blakeley/istockphoto.com; Canadian Rockies © Matt Naylor/istockphoto.com; Vancouver © Rick Jones/istockphoto.com; Whistler Resort © Gary Blakeley/istockphoto.com; Toronto © John Pitcher/istockphoto.com; Woman's silhouette © Dip2000/Dreamstime.com; Man's silhouette © Alexkalina/Dreamstime.com; Hat © Greenland/Dreamstime.com; pp56–57: Goose, Left © Drflet/istockphoto.com; Goose, Middle © Charles Brutlag/istockphoto.com; Goose, Right © Noegruts/Dreamstime.com; Radio Tower © PKruger/Dreamstime.com; Headphones © 7nuit/istockphoto.com; p58: Beaver © Vchphoto/Dreamstime.com; Boom Box © Tyler Derden/Dreamstime.com; p62: Victrola © Catzovescu/Dreamstime.com; Goose © Drflet/istockphoto.com; p72: Beaver © Shootalot/Dreamstime.com; Sound Board © Anikasalsera/Dreamstime.com; p77 Vegas Sign © Jlvdream/Dreamstime.com; pp80–81: Beaver © Steve Raubenstine/istockphoto.com; Bottles © Jalifree/istockphoto.com; p82: Dollar © Stillfix/Dreamstime.com; p86: Washington Monument © Nedens/Dreamstime.com; Canoe © Eric Naud/istockphoto.com; Beaver © Shootalot/Dreamstime.com; Goose © Charles Brutlag/istockphoto.com; Beaver © Photawa/Dreamstime.com; p87: Telephone © Winston Davidian/istockphoto.com; Goose © Charles Brutlag/istockphoto.com pp90–91: Earth and Hubble Telescope © James Benet/istockphoto.com; Canadarm 2. Canadian Space Agency. www.space.gc.ca; Goose © Charles Brutlag/istockphoto.com; p99: Tent © Ene/istockphoto.com; Beaver, Left © Steve Raubenstine/istockphoto.com; Beaver, Right © Simon Phipps/istockphoto.com p102: Beaver © Vchphoto/Dreamstime.com; Drink © Rebecca Ellis/istockphoto.com; Clam © Kevin Thomas/istockphoto.com; p104: Beaver © Photawa/Dreamstime.com; Eagle © Stevemcsweeny/Dreamstime.com; Bottle © Ljupco/Dreamstime.com; p105: Goose © Mmphotography/Dreamstime.com; Casks © Razvanjp/Dreamstime.com; pp106–107 Moose © Reinhardt/Dreamstime.com; Sport silhouettes © Goce/Dreamstime.com; p110: Statue of Liberty © BurningLiquid/Dreamstime.com; p111: Hockey field © Amarius5/Dreamstime.com; p112: Basketball Hoop © Genrommel/Dreamstime.com; p115: Baseball Bat © Ljupko/Dreamstime.com; Moose © Spydr.Dreamstime.com; p119: Beaver © Simon Phipps/istockphoto.com; Eagle © Do Hoai Nam/istockphoto.com; p120: Beaver © Shootalot/Dreamstime.com; Beaver © Vchphoto/Dreamstime.com; Typewriter © Narvikk/istockphoto.com; Coffee Cup © Charles Taylor/istockphoto.com

CONTENTS

THE SHOCKING TRUTH

Let's just start with the obvious: Everybody loves Canadians.

Of course they do! Canadians are laid-back, funny, and cute; they enjoy drinking beer, apologizing, and playing hockey with their friends. Their accents are charming, subtle, and, come to think of it, kind of sexy (who doesn't like an elongated *O*?). Their dress favors cozy, low-profile plaids; they tend not to complain about freezing weather; and though they've been known to eat moose and made a beaver their national mascot, they still somehow seem more enlightened than the rest of us. They exude a quiet confidence, and it's not just that they've successfully mastered the metric system. No, clearly, there's something else afoot.

Naturally you've heard people say things like, "Canadians are so cool," or "Those Canadians sure are doing things right." And most likely you've found yourself at a party where a friend leans over, almost spilling her Molson's, and excitedly says, "I met someone new—he's smart, funny, and best of all, he's Canadian!" And be honest, how often do you find yourself thinking, "Wow, I wish *I* was Canadian"? It's OK. We all do it. We understand. And we're here to let you in on a little secret that just might blow your world wide open:

PASSPORT

*United States
of America*

EXHIBIT EH?

You already are Canadian. You just don't know it.

"No way," you might think, "I'm American!" Well, yes . . . and no. You may be technically American, according to your government-issued paperwork. But the truth (can you handle the truth?) is that your everyday life, in arguably the most powerful country in the world, is influenced, controlled, and subtly (yet benevolently) manipulated—day in and day *oot*—by Canada.

Oh sure, Canada has cleverly cultivated its politely cooperative, self-effacing reputation as agreeable "Canucks" and even bumbling "hosers" while its people live quietly among us, all the while masterminding a total domination of the United States (and therefore the world) in true Canadian form. No flashy coups, no showing off. Instead, their work is done through the movies we watch, the songs we listen to, the jokes that make us laugh, the sports we play, the political analysts we trust, the household products we use. Yes, the industries and the economics that make America what it is are all quietly and efficiently controlled by that master puppeteer, Canada.

Why? Well, it's genius. Canadians get to live in a quiet, clean, relaxed country where they're envied, patted on the back, and generally thought of as adorable—when all the while, they are a power broker by proxy. They're able to claim the good for themselves (international peacekeeping, affordable prescriptions, universal health care, tasty beer) and slough off the dregs to America (war, economic colonialism, pollution, Britney Spears). They get to watch millions of people do their bidding. And they get to launch their grand experiments and see the results from a comfortable perch up north. Did you really think that Canada was just hanging out up there, smoking weed and curling? As they say in Quebec, *Au contraire, mes amis.*

Still skeptical? Consider for a moment a typical "American" day at home. You get up, turn on the light, and make yourself some eggs Benedict. You pull up the zipper on your jacket to take the garbage bags to the curb, pick up the newspaper, and turn on the lawn sprinklers on your way back inside. You put your child in the Jolly Jumper so your hands are free to answer the telephone while you make the pablum. Later you grab a ginger ale and a chocolate bar and turn on the basketball game, while your family settles in to play some Yahtzee. Then sometime that evening, say while listening to Hot Hot Heat or Neil Young, tracking the hockey scores, checking your BlackBerry, and flipping between Kiefer Sutherland on *24* and a documentary on penguins on TV, it hits you.

"Canada!" you exclaim, upending your TV tray of frozen fish fillets, instant mashed potatoes, and Labatt's. "Good God, they're behind everything!"

Suddenly, it becomes crystal clear. The goalie mask is removed, as it were, and as if you had Superman's X-ray vision, everything is revealed. You look around and see Canada everywhere. You run back to the kitchen and pull out the package from that morning's meal. Bacon. CANADIAN bacon! You see that Canada is controlling every aspect of your day-to-day life—and everyone else's in America, too. If you're not yet convinced, read on. In these pages you will see, as surely as William Shatner is the greatest entertainer of our time, that you are living not in the U.S. of A., but in the U.S. of *Eh*?

THE BIG PICTURE

> "Be extremely subtle, even to the point of formless-
> ness. Be extremely mysterious, even to the point of
> soundlessness. Thereby you can be the director
> of the opponent's fate." —Sun Tzu, *The Art of War*

Once we began to realize that Canada is in control of everything, we wondered how this could be. How did Canada
come to this position of power—with no one even noticing?
Although crafty Canadians, like the Freemasons, do most
of their work cloaked in a veil of secrecy, we managed to
uncover a range of suspicious events that together indi-
cate the shadowy outlines of a Canadian conspiracy that's
centuries old.

First, consider Canada's seemingly inexplicable ability
to keep unwanted intruders out of its great land, with a
surprising lack of militia or bloodshed. Somehow, even with
Canada's relatively wee population, no interlopers have
ever been able to grab all those valuable purple mountains,
fruited plains, and amber waves of grain. How has Canada
so easily rebuffed not one, but two invasion attempts by
the ostensibly more powerful and populous U.S.? And why
is it that no one has even tried to take them over since? It's
hard to explain—unless Canada is pulling some serious and
secret strings. The evidence we've gathered suggests that
Canadian operations have been based on a two-pronged

approach: First, divert all attention to its brash neighbors south of the forty-ninth parallel (who are only too happy to act out). Second, craft an image that pulls the wool over everyone's eyes like a Hudson's Bay blanket. Then you're free to execute any plot you like.

> "Canada is a place of infinite promise. We like the people, and if one ever had to emigrate, this would be the destination, not the U.S.A. The hills, lakes, and forests make it a place of peace and repose of the mind, such as one never finds in the U.S.A."
> —John Maynard Keynes

Canada is clearly the most desirable country on the continent. It has plentiful natural resources, a sheer size advantage (see map, page 19), and a limitless supply of cocktail ice. Those in the know have considered it the better property since before America was even taken seriously; consider that the Vikings, no dummies on the exploration front, completely skipped the U.S. and came to Canada a full five hundred years before Columbus reached the Americas. After Columbus got himself turned around and almost "discovered" Canada before landing in the U.S., Canada realized that it had been a very close call, and seized the opportunity to keep its neighborhood from going to hell. It was time to push everybody south.

Starting at that moment, and continuing to this day, clever Canada has resisted the urge to toot its own horn, keeping a low profile to mask its plentiful riches and awesome power and instead letting its southern neighbor hog the spotlight.

Sure, Canadians are known for their modesty in social situations, but who would've guessed that this modesty, this quickness to apologize, this friendly, down-home deference, has always been part of a larger secret plan? Beginning way back when everyone was in a New World frenzy, Canada shrewdly took a backseat and let America boast about its available land, brave settlers, and the "American dream," while perpetuating the false rumors of Canada as an inhospitable place of igloos and ice.

YOU BE THE JUDGE

Although American schoolchildren are taught that the word "Canada" is derived from the Iroquois word for "peaceful village," those in the know say Canada is an acronym for its true purpose:

Central Annex for North American Domination A (Eh?)

The result? The buzz was all about America. Immigrants came to crowd the lower part of the continent, and with plenty of room, no suspicion, and time on its hands, Canada was free to begin taking charge, with no one the wiser. The U.S. was perfectly poised for its role as a patsy—it was nicely situated nearby, it was booming with new hard-working people, and it seemed like a hot little up-and-comer where money could be made and things were happening. It was, for Canada, "the land of opportunity."

Lessons in Geography

Igloo (*ig'loo*)

This typical Canadian house is a modest dome-shaped dwelling made with bricks of snow, the only building material available to the poor souls forced to call the freezing cold wilderness that comprises most of Canada "home."

y
ut
ve
p.

Acting as behind-the-scenes master, it would be relatively easy to get a large piece of that American pie—while still living in serene and spacious comfort—as long as Canada kept to an under-the-radar style that was virtually risk-free. So, while the United States got into skirmish after skirmish, and continued to show off, Canada sat back, played some hockey, and formulated its plans.

> "Speak softly and carry a big stick; you will go far."
> —Theodore Roosevelt

That's not to say that Canada wasn't willing to flex its muscles when it had to. For instance, when U.S. upstarts decided to invade Canada in 1775, they were easily rebuffed. (Conveniently soon thereafter, 50,000 Americans voted with their feet and fled north, ready to become Canadian double-agents.) When the U.S. tried invading *again* during the War of 1812, they failed, again, and Canada reminded the U.S. who was boss, this time burning down the White House and seizing Detroit (which it graciously returned, good sports to the end). Point made, Canada found it unnecessary, and counterproductive, to enter into open conflict with the U.S.; that's not its style. After all, a measure of true power is the ability to wield it without drawing attention to your own actions, secure in your dominance while allowing those you secretly control to believe they are acting freely. It's smarter, and safer, to rule as the silent puppeteer. So, after handily brushing aside two American invasions, Canada has played nice with its neighbor, perpetuated its laid-back image, and downplayed its secret strength (to this day, it has a volunteer army of a mere 64,000, which leaves many more able-bodied Canadians available to do the real work of running the entire continent—and going for beer runs).

This buddy-buddy attitude isn't just a great cover for Canada's true mission; it has also resulted in tangible benefits that directly further Canada's cause, not the least of which is the creation of the world's largest undefended border (between Canada and the U.S.). This genius Canadian coup—offered as a polite suggestion—was easily agreed to by the U.S. because, hey, why bother all those nice, polite Canadians who want to come back and forth into America, undetected? What's the harm? Meanwhile, no one stops to question why a full 75 percent of Canadians live at or near the border, where they can swoop down at a moment's notice, the perfect perch for both infiltrating the U.S. and monitoring their investments. (Can it really be mere coincidence that Canada's two largest cities, Toronto and Montreal, as well as its federal capital of Ottawa, actually lie well *south* of the forty-ninth parallel?)

YOU'VE BEEN CANUCKED

He-man American writer Ernest Hemingway's secret schoolboy crush on Canada was revealed when he recklessly wrote the poem "I Like Canadians," and then tried to pass it under the classroom desk by publishing it on the down-low in the *Toronto Star* in 1923.

CANADA:
LARGE AND IN CHARGE

TYPICAL MAP OF NORTH AMERICA USED IN AMERICAN CLASSROOMS

While Canada is made to appear smaller on maps in the United States so as not to freak out Americans with its obvious dominance, it's actually significantly bigger—350,000 sqare kilometers bigger (about the size of a 600 square kilometer rumpus room) and second in national territory only to Russia.

OTTAWA

MAP OF NORTH AMERICA TO ACTUAL SCALE.

🍁 NOTE THAT OTTAWA, CANADA'S CAPITAL CITY, LIES SOUTH OF THE 49TH PARALLEL.

Canada plays it cool with other countries, too. When it came time to sever ties to Mother England, Canadians kept their cards close to their vests. Rather than doing the whole American-style "rockets' red glare" fanfare, Canada took a more subtle route and therefore avoided arousing ire or suspicion. Canada wasn't officially declared "one dominion under the name Canada" on the world stage until July 1, 1867, and it didn't debut its own (stunning) maple leaf flag

"I'M SORRY." *BUT ARE THEY?*

One of the more charming cultural predilections of Canadians is to apologize at the drop of a toque ("hat" in American). But consider what linguists have long recognized: apologizing doesn't mean that you're actually *sorry.* As an ingratiating means of resolving conflict and keeping things on an even keel, it can simply be tactically expedient, especially if one is apologizing from a position of power. Consider the satirical "truly Canadian apology to the U.S.A." delivered by comedian Colin Mochrie on the Canadian TV show *This Hour Has 22 Minutes,* which says in part:

"On behalf of Canadians everywhere, I'd like to offer an apology to the United States of America. . . . I'm sorry about our softwood lumber. Just because we have more trees than you doesn't give us the right to sell you lumber that's cheaper and better than your own. . . . I'm sorry we beat you at Olympic hockey . . . [and] I'm sorry that we're constantly apologizing for things in a passive-aggressive way, which is really a thinly veiled criticism."

until *1965.* How subtle is *that*? Because they took thei
time to quietly, politely break up with Britain without
feathers, Canadians could work on their undercover plans
for years without raising a single eyebrow. People didn't
even think of Canada as its own country, much less one to
worry about. It's a tactic that works well to this day. In fact,
many Americans—when they remember Canada at all—still
believe it's part of England. After all, the Queen is on the
money and Canadians still use lots of cute British phrases
and spellings. It's these sorts of thoughtful touches that reveal
the brilliance of Canada's plan: who could suspect someone
who still "favours" sitting on a "chesterfield"?

> "Canada is the linchpin of the English-speaking
> world." —Sir Winston Churchill

While the U.S. is its main target, Canada has charmed the
rest of the world with its helpful, accommodating demeanor
and quiet political enlightenment that allow for its stealthy
progress. Like the easygoing guy who everyone wants at
the party, Canada is always invited to the political table; it
has easily fallen into the role of knitter-together of allies and
allegiances without making enemies—an enviable position
that only helps in furthering its own causes. Canada is a
founding member of the U.N. and the G8, which keeps it
in the mix with the brasher world leaders, and is also a
founding signatory of NATO, the Ottawa Mine-Ban Treaty,
and the Kyoto Protocol for greenhouse gas emissions.
Canadian legal scholar and jurist John Peters Humphrey,
while acting as the first director of the Human Rights

Division of the United Nations, was also the principal drafter of the Universal Declaration of Human Rights.

And while Canada has been quietly leading by example as the U.S. inches toward its own Canadian-style higher standard of living, it has notably avoided using overt political action in America the same way it shrugged off outright annexation (too obvious, and unnecessary). Since Americans don't generally hold their politicians in high regard, why muck about with such negative association? Celebrity culture is the driving force in the U.S. media, so control of it is a direct route to the American psyche and keeping the U.S. in line. Sure, Canada has carefully planted economic and industrial giants in America (from John Kenneth Galbraith to Dow Chemical, see "How You Live") to keep things humming along according to plan. But Canada saw that effectively monopolizing the everyday "American" media machine—movies, radio, TV, communication devices, household products—would be the best way to control the continent in a new era. Canada didn't skip a beat, and quickly jumped in to take over these burgeoning industries and keep hold of the reins. Canadian influence exerted from the Homeland and Canadian operatives working within the U.S. have been quietly calling the shots and shaping every aspect of our normal "American" lives, and they have been ruling the United States this way ever since.

"We hold these truths to be self-evident, that all men are created equal, that they are endowed by their Creator with certain unalienable Rights, that among these are Life, Liberty and the pursuit of Happiness

WHAT YOU

WATCH

CANADA
Edmonton
Vancouver
Saskatoon
Calgary
Regina
Victoria
Tacoma
Portland
Seattle
Spokane
NORTH
Yakima
Great Falls
Salem
Eugene
Butte
UNITED STATES OF AMERICA
Boise
Billings
Fargo
Salt Lake City
Rapid City
San Francisco
Sacramento
Ogden
Oakland
Price
AMERICA
San Jose
Los Angeles
Denver
Las Vegas
San Diego
Pueblo
Long Beach
Kansas City
Tijuana
Albuquerque
Phoenix
Tucson
Dallas
BAJA
Hermosillo
Austin
Alijos Rock
Monterey
CENTRAL
Culiacan
Mazatlan
AMERICA
MEXICO
Guadalajara
San luis Potos
Tampico
Leon
Manzanillo
Mexico City
Acapulco

OPERATION
PROPACANADA

"Canada's fourth-largest city is Los Angeles. More
Canadians live there than in Ottawa or Calgary or
Edmonton or Quebec City." —Douglas Coupland

As everyone knows, the key to controlling a culture—its
politics, its hopes and dreams, its sense of self and what is
possible—is to control its media. In the modern world, the
influence of media is incalculable, and arguably the biggest
jewel in that crown is the movies. The magic of movies can
sway people like nothing else, so it's no surprise that Hollywood, the most American of cultural phenomena, is dubbed
the "dream factory"—shaping American (and international)
taste in fashion, music, cars, cuisine, romance, and ideals
of beauty. For generations, it has been teaching us who
the good guys are, who the bad guys are, when to cheer,
and even who's worth kissing. It's an industry full of razzle-
dazzle, glamour, mystery, and money. We track its ups and
downs via box office numbers, glossy movie magazines, and
celebrity news, and politicians intone about its social and
political influence as it holds Americans from coast to coast
in its thrall. Of course, it was invented by Canada.

YOU'VE BEEN CANUCKED

Not only did Canadian actresses dominate the box office for much of Hollywood's golden age, the Academy Award for best actress was bestowed upon three different Canadian women in a row:

1929 – Mary Pickford in *Coquette*
1930 – Norma Shearer in *The Divorcée*
1931 – Marie Dressler in *Min and Bill*

The founders of MGM, United Artists, and Warner Bros.? Canadian. The best actress Academy Award winners, three years in a row, during the heyday of the silver screen? Canadian. The "beauty who charmed the beast" in *King Kong*? Canadian. The two actresses dubbed "America's First Movie Star" and "America's Sweetheart"? Canadian.

Canada launched Hollywood back in the golden age of film, kicking off its grand plan to influence and distract Americans by strategically putting some key players in place:

THE MOGUL Canadian studio head Louis B. Mayer was Hollywood's most legendary powerhouse and founder of MGM. Mayer established the "star system," ensuring that Americans would faithfully follow his actors' every move (laying the groundwork for *E!*, *US Weekly*, supermarket tabloids, and other enduring American distractions), and, handpicking Canadian operatives like Norma Shearer (see at right) to become household names. He's also credited with rallying Americans when they needed it most, releasing the audaciously expensive and galvanizing *Ben Hur* at the height of the Depression, and by making MGM the only studio that still paid dividends during the 1930s (perhaps by using Canadian loonies)?

THE COMPETITION So as not to have the whole town obviously run by Mayer, Canadian brothers Jack and Sam Warner—a.k.a. Warner Bros.—established a "competing" studio, making the first "talkie" (*The Jazz Singer*) and later diversifying into a television and music powerhouse.

THE MOVIE STAR The woman dubbed "America's First Movie Star" was Canadian Florence Lawrence. Somehow, no one noticed.

THE SWEETHEART Canadian Mary Pickford was handed one of the first movie studio contracts in 1908, and it made her the most famous woman in the world. She reigned for nearly twenty-five years as the undisputed queen of the screen, an Oscar winner and endlessly likeable actress known as (yes . . .) "America's Sweetheart." She increased her influence by marrying matinee idol Douglas Fairbanks and befriending Charlie Chaplin, with whom she created United Artists, an "actor-run" (read: Canadian-run) studio. She also held court at her legendary estate and mover-and-shaker hangout Pickfair, where she whispered in the ears of Hollywood's most powerful. Though Americans thought of her as their own, she did slip up once in an interview in which she was quoted as saying, "At least once a month I dream I'm back in Toronto."

THE PRESTIGE ACTRESS

Oscar-winning powerhouse Norma Shearer (daughter of a Mountie) was the Meryl Streep of her day. She was the Canadian lead of the heavy-hitting trifecta created by Mayer, which included Shearer, Greta Garbo, and Joan Crawford, together the biggest earners not just at MGM, but in all of Hollywood.

THE B-MOVIE SIREN

Oscar wins and tabloid dreams are all fine, if a little showy. Recognizing a deficiency in its B-picture coverage, Canada dispatched blonde bombshell/operative Fay Wray to play a string of scream-queen roles before getting her big break in *King Kong*. The big ape's adoration for the Canadian beauty eventually drives him up the side of that iconic American skyscraper, from which he plummets—literally falling in love with Canada.

YOU BE THE JUDGE

The Empire State Building went dark for fifteen minutes when Fay Wray died. But was it actually Quebec—major supplier of electricity to NYC and the eastern seaboard—who turned out the lights?

THE BIG TAKEOVER:
MODERN MOVIES AND TV

Canadian domination of the big screen carries on to this day, with Canadian operatives pulling the strings on blockbusters such as *Titanic*, *Star Wars*, *Terminator*, and *Shrek*—more on this soon—but come midcentury, when it became clear that Americans liked being glued to the tube, Canada expanded its media monopoly to television. (Those in the know claim that "TV" actually stands for Toronto-Vancouver.) And in doing so it would inaugurate a campaign that proved so successful it would become the hallmark of Canada's media operations from then on: Canada would seduce America as it would best charm a woman—it would make her laugh.

The landmark "American" TV program *The Ed Sullivan Show* was Canada's first target. It was the perfect test case, the highest-rated show and most widely-shared television experience of the day, around which the greatest number of Americans cozied up with their TV trays (laden with fish sticks) every Sunday night through the '50s and '60s. And who, in Ed Sullivan's heyday, was the number-one act? Of course it was Canadian comedy duo Johnny Wayne and Frank Shuster, known as "Wayne and Shuster." Their intellectual slapstick was a huge hit with audiences, and the pair appeared a record sixty-seven times over eleven years, with complete creative freedom over their sketches. In 1962 and '63, both *Motion Picture Daily* and *Television Today* ranked the duo as the best comedy team in America, and they stunned U.S. network executives by declining their own show in order to stay in their homeland/headquarters, Canada. Operation Comedy was off to a smashing start.

Fast-forward a bit to 1975. In addition to placing Canadian comedians on established American shows, Canada would go on to create its own training program/base camp on American television, run by Canadians, written by Canadians, and featuring Canadian actors who could easily bounce between the small and big screens, inventing characters who would insinuate themselves into the general consciousness

YOU BE THE JUDGE

The Canadian one-dollar coin, which features a picture of a loon, is a "loonie." The Canadian two-dollar coin is a "toonie." When Warner Bros. launched an animated cartoon series in 1930, playing in theaters and eventually on television, and spawning classic "American" cartoon pals such as Daffy Duck, Porky Pig, Bugs Bunny, and countless others, what did they call it? "Looney Tunes." (Note the sly alternate spelling.) Playful animated entertainment for generations of children, or subtle indoctrination for a future of handling Canadian currency?

and basically infiltrate the minds of anyone hardy enough to stay up until midnight. Enter *Saturday Night Live,* helmed by Canadian Lorne Michaels (who was also the producer of Canada's *Kids in the Hall* comedy show). Canadian comedians including Dan Ackroyd, Martin Short, Phil Hartman, and Mike Myers shot to stardom on the weekly program, using it as a launching pad for later film conquests—all according to the master plan. Hit movies born from *SNL* (and starring Canadians) as the show developed included *Coneheads* and *The Blues Brothers* (starring Ackroyd), *The Three Amigos* (starring Short), and the *Wayne's World* series (starring Myers). Meanwhile, when not busy counting their money, Canadians everywhere got a good laugh as ridiculous phrases like "Party on, Garth" and "Excellent!" became ubiquitous in the modern American vernacular. Canuck comedy operatives were also placed on other shows, diversifying their portfolio into America's *In Living Color* (Jim Carrey) and the Canadian/American sketch comedy series *SCTV* (John Candy, Martin Short, Eugene Levy, Andrea Martin, Rick Moranis, Catherine O'Hara, Dave Thomas).

YOU'VE BEEN CANUCKED

Unassuming comic Frank Shuster reigns supreme as a Canadian propaganda machine. Besides his own influential comedy duo, he is the father-in-law of heir apparent Lorne Michaels and the cousin of Joe Shuster, the creator of Superman (see "Superman, the Greatest Canadian Hero," page 100)!

EXHIBIT EH?

LAUGHTER:
THE OPIATE OF THE MASSES?

Tripping some of the same neural triggers as addictive narcotics, laughter stimulates the pleasure centers of the brain. Here are some Canadian funny folks you've probably heard of. Have they been simply making you laugh, or have they been *controlling your mind*?

JOHN CANDY   MIKE MEYERS   PHIL HARTMAN

DAN ACKROYD   JIM CARREY   EUGENE LEVY

RICK MORANIS   SAMANTHA BEE   HOWIE MANDEL

CATHERINE O'HARA   LESLIE NIELSEN   RICH LITTLE

WILL ARNETT   SETH ROGEN   CAROLINE RHEA

NIA VARDALOS   MARTIN SHORT   DAVE FOLEY

TOMMY CHONG   LORNE GREENE

(yes, he was funny
and kicked ass on *Bonanza*)

LAUGHING
ALL THE WAY TO THE BANK

While they make you laugh and control your every thought, Canadian comics also rake in the American dollars—funneling the dough back to Canada to train more operatives.

Jim Carrey: One of the highest-paid actors in Hollywood, his big movies include *The Mask, Ace Ventura: Pet Detective, The Truman Show, Eternal Sunshine of the Spotless Mind,* and *Bruce Almighty,* the latter of which became the third highest grossing live-action comedy of all time with about $242 million in U.S. box office receipts.

Mike Meyers: Best known for the *Wayne's World*, *Austin Powers*, and *Shrek* series, his *Shrek 2* earned $436 million in U.S. box office receipts alone, making it the No. 3 top grossing U.S. movie of all time—beating out American classics *E.T., Pirates of the Caribbean*, and *Star Wars: Episode I*.

WHAT'S ON TV? *CANADA!*

Over time, Canada strategically expanded its reach, infiltrating not only comedies, but dramas, action series, animation, game shows, and the longest-running sitcom of all time, *The Simpsons*.

24: Canadian Kiefer Sutherland keeps America safe at any cost. (Sutherland's TV daughter is also played by a Canadian (see page 53), and his real-life Canadian pop Donald was *M.A.S.H.*'s Hawkeye in the original Robert Altman film.)

Arrested Development: This caustic, critically acclaimed sitcom featured Toronto-born comedian Will Arnett (who happens to be married to Amy Poehler, who works for Lorne Michaels on *SNL*) and Jason Bateman, who may be American—but is married to Paul Anka's daughter Amanda, making him a Canadian-in-law.

Baywatch: In which Canadian bombshell and *Playboy* Playmate Pamela Anderson ran in slow motion into the dreams of millions.

YOU'VE BEEN CANUCKED

Fishing line, chewing gum, a paper clip, and . . . Canada. Good ol' American ingenuity was celebrated every week on *MacGyver*—but the show was both filmed and produced in Canada (and note the many appearances by Dan Ackroyd!).

Beverly Hills, 90210: Canadian Jason Priestley was the token nice guy among typical California brats.

Bonanza and the original Battlestar Galactica: Lorne Greene lorded over both the Western frontier *and* outer space in these American TV classics.

YOU'VE BEEN CANUCKED

Art Linkletter, the pride of Moose Jaw, Saskatchewan, was the host of two of the longest-running shows in American broadcast history: *House Party*, which ran on CBS for twenty-five years, and *People Are Funny,* on NBC for nineteen years.

Family Ties: Cute Canadian Michael J. Fox's Alex P. Keaton bought into the American dream to comic effect (with Fox further wading into the amusements of the U.S. political milieu in *Spin City*); he also starred in the hugely successful *Back to the Future* films.

Friends: The highest-grossing American sitcom starred Matthew Perry, son of former Canadian prime minister Pierre Trudeau's press secretary (and the former Old Spice hunk!).

Grey's Anatomy: A hit brought to life by Canada's Sandra Oh (who also rocked the Oscar-winning *Sideways*).

In Living Color: Jim Carrey's training ground and launching pad to future Hollywood hits.

Jeopardy: Who has been kindly reminding Americans to phrase their answer in the form of a question since 1984? Clever Canadian Alex Trebek (whose game show success was preceded by fellow Canadians Monty Hall on *Let's Make a Deal* and Jim Perry on *Card Sharks*). Today, *Deal or No Deal* is presided over by Toronto-born Howie Mandel.

Late Night With David Letterman: "Orchestrated" in more ways than one by "sidekick" and Thunder Bay native Paul Shaffer . . . just as *Late Night with Conan O'Brien* is controlled by Canadian executive producer Lorne Michaels. (When not busy making Letterman a success, Shaffer has served as maestro for several "American" institutions, from the Blues Brothers to the Rock and Roll Hall of Fame, also serving as chairman of the American Red Cross recruiting drive. But really, what legacy can compare to his penning the '80s dance hit "It's Raining Men"? Hallelujah!)

YOU BE THE JUDGE

Why was Lorne Michaels the best man at American comedian Steve Martin's recent wedding? Is it because Martin honed his early stand-up career in Canada, where he was indoctrinated as a sort of Canadian Manchurian candidate, ready to play his part when called upon later as part of the Master Plan?

YOU BE THE JUDGE

Canadian Jim Carrey had a breakthrough dramatic performance in *The Truman Show,* about a clueless guy who didn't realize someone else was holding the puppet strings and controlling his life—a clever metaphor for the real-life Canadian-American power dynamic?

Lost: Canadian hottie Evangeline Lilly is a key reason that people are fascinated by this mysterious island.

Newsradio: This '90s sitcom featured the talents of Canadian *Kids in the Hall* comic Dave Foley and the beloved Phil Hartman.

Party of Five: Ontario-born Neve Campbell was a fetching orphan in this teenage guilty pleasure, and would later go on to help the *Scream* films rake in more than $366 million worldwide.

Perry Mason: Canadian Raymond Burr embodied the honor of the American legal system in this long-running lawyer drama, later going on to snare Yankee criminals in *Ironside*.

Saturday Night Live: A staging ground for Canadian comedy operatives for more than thirty years.

Scrubs: Ottawa-born Sarah Chalke is the resident cutie on this long-running popular sitcom.

Sex and the City: The award-winning HBO series got its super-boost of sex appeal from Canadian Kim Cattrall's Samantha (who was sexy in the Canadian flick *Porky's* years earlier, and would later give Americans a steamy education in her books *Satisfaction: The Art of the Female Orgasm* and *Sexual Intelligence*).

The Simpsons: Matt Groening, creator of TV's longest-running sitcom, may not be Canadian—but several of his writers and producers are, and according to Groening, so is hero Homer Simpson (who has been known to drink maple syrup for breakfast).

Star Trek: William Shatner's legendary Captain James Tiberius Kirk, the pride of Montreal, always got the job done and got the girl—creating a legion of Trekkies who would dream of following his example. And who did he trust to keep the ship going? Canadian James "Scotty" Doohan.

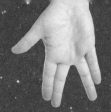

SHAT FACTS!

Simply Captain Kirk? Hardly. Canadian super-entertainer William Shatner has enriched and shaped the lives of Americans through platforms and activities as diverse as television, music, film, theater, books, advertising, and charity work. Behold the true King of All Media.

FACT His first big-screen appearance came in a 1951 movie entitled *The Butler's Night Off* and, in 1954, he made his TV debut as "Ranger Bill" in the Canadian version of *Howdy Doody*.

FACT *How William Shatner Changed the World*, a two-hour special aired on Discovery Canada in 2005, revealed how the Shat—and his work on the U.S.S. *Enterprise* on the TV show *Star Trek* and the first seven spin-off films—is responsible for many breakthroughs in science and technology in the United States, from flip phones to medicalimaging. The special was based on Shatner's book *I'm Working on That*, and featured interviews with some of the famous inventors who were inspired by *Star Trek*.

FACT The Students University Centre at Shat's alma mater, McGill University in Montreal, is unofficially named after him. ("Meet you at the Shat!")

FACT Shat produces and hosts the annual Hollywood Charity Horse Show, which he founded in 1990, raising more than $1.25 million for children's charities such as Ahead With Horses, L.A.'s BEST, and Children's Museum of Los Angeles. Shat himself is an expert horseman, who also breeds and shows American Saddlebreds (coincidence?)

FACT In January 2006, Shat sold his kidney stone for $25,000 USD to benefit Habitat for Humanity.

FACT At the 2005 *AFI Life Achievement Award: A Tribute to George Lucas* show, William Shatner—joined by a group of dancing stormtroopers—serenaded George Lucas with the Canuck classic "My Way" by Paul Anka, to big laughs.

FACT After being robbed of Emmys over the years for his work on *Star Trek* and *Rescue 911*, Shat was nominated for his guest-starring role in *3rd Rock from the Sun*, and scored Emmys for his work on *The Practice* and *Boston Legal*.

FACT Shat is actually—of all things—a classically trained Shakespeare man.

FACT Shat received a star on the Hollywood Walk of Fame in 1983. He was inducted into the Broadcasting & Cable Hall of Fame in 2005, and the Television Academy's Hall of Fame in 2006, recognizing "a lifetime of excellence and special recognition for those who have made significant contributions that will leave an indelible mark on the television business."

FACT Shat's original *Star Trek* series only aired three seasons, beginning in 1966. *T.J. Hooker*, on the other hand, aired for four, beginning in 1982.

FACT According to producer Debra Hill, a Halloween mask in Shatner's likeness was painted white and used as the mask of Michael Myers in the original *Halloween* (1978). Interestingly, the killer's name is the same as a certain Canuck comedian . . .

FACT Shat is also immortalized by Adam Sandler in "The Hanukkah Song" ("You don't need Deck the Halls or Jingle Bell Rock/When you can spin a dreidel with Captain Kirk and Mr. Spock").

FACT Riverside, Iowa, the hometown of Shat's alter-ego Capt. Kirk, is known by hardcore Trekkies as "the other Kirkland" (as Kirkland, Canada, is a few miles from Shat's hometown of Montreal, Quebec).

FACT Shatner's daughter Lisabeth wrote the script for the *T.J. Hooker* episode "Partners in Death" (1986). (She was also Miss Golden Globe 1985.)

FACT "Nightmare at 20,000 Feet," *The Twilight Zone* episode starring Shat, has long been considered by fans as one of the best of the series and was paid homage to by being remade in the 1983 film version.

FACT Shat's 1968 album *The Transformed Man* helped to win him his lucrative deal as the Priceline.com spokesman. An employee of the ad agency hired by Priceline had fond memories of the album, which he listened to in his childhood. In 2004, Shat released the autobiographical album *Has Been*, a collaboration with Ben Folds.

QUOTH THE SHAT

"I'm not a Starfleet commander, or T.J. Hooker. I don't live on Starship NCC-1701 or own a phaser. I speak English and French, not Klingon! I drink Labatt's, not Romulan ale! My name is William Shatner, and I am Canadian!"

FACT Shat has appeared in episodes of five different series with Leonard Nimoy: *The Man from U.N.C.L.E.*, *Star Trek*, *Star Trek: The Animated Series*, *T.J. Hooker*, and *Futurama*. They also appeared in a TV commercial for Priceline together.

FACT Shat's clipped, dramatic narration, peppered with dramatic pauses, is often referred to as "Shatnerian." He's man enough to admit that those dramatic pauses in Kirk's speeches were the result of trying to remember his next line.

FACT His 1986 *Saturday Night Live* quote to rabid fans, "Get a Life," was infamous and inspired a 1999 book of the same name. He is the author of several biographical books, comic books, and *Star Trek* novels.

FACT Shat's favorite *Star Trek* episode is "The Devil in the Dark."

FACT *Parlez-vous francais?* Shat does, fluently.

AMERICA'S
MOST TRUSTED
SOURCE FOR NEWS?

Samantha Bee: Could *The Daily Show with Jon Stewart* be that funny without a Canadian on board? As if!

Peter Jennings: One of the "big three" (with Brokaw and Rather) until his death in 2005, Canadian Jennings was the sole anchor of ABC's *World News Tonight* for more than twenty years.

Arthur Kent: Seeking to increase news viewership by American women, Canada sent "Scud Stud" Kent to the rescue during the Gulf War.

Norm MacDonald: *SNL* never had a funnier deadpan deliverer of "Weekend Update."

Robert MacNeil: Born in Montreal, raised in Halifax, the journalist, author, and longtime coanchor of *The MacNeil/Lehrer Report* and *The MacNeil/Lehrer NewsHour* is an officer in the Order of Canada, which recognizes lifetime contributions of Canadian civilians.

John Roberts: After fourteen years as chief White House correspondent and news anchor for CBS, Roberts now anchors CNN's flagship morning program *"American" Morning.* (In Canada, he was just an MTV VJ!)

Morley Safer: A *60 Minutes* correspondent for thirty-five years, Safer famously angered President Lyndon B. Johnson by reporting the truth in Vietnam, prompting the explanation that he was "not a communist, just Canadian." (Johnson replied, "Well, I knew he wasn't an American.")

YOU'VE BEEN CANUCKED

Canada invented both the documentary film genre (with *Nanook of the North* in 1922) and the IMAX movie system, which James Cameron utilized in his deepsea exploration documentary *Aliens of the Deep.*

LIGHTS, CAMERA, *CANADA!*

What's the highest-grossing movie of all time—by far—with over $600 million in U.S. box office alone, and almost $2 billion worldwide? The movie that also won a record eleven Academy Awards? Yep, it's *Titanic*—directed, written, and painstakingly crafted by James Cameron, a Canadian. (Oh, and the Oscar-winning theme song that went along with it, "My Heart Will Go On"? It was sung by Canadian Céline Dion, natch; see page 78). And that's not all Cameron has been up to; he was also behind mega-movies like the *Terminator* series, *Rambo, Aliens, The Abyss,* and *True Lies.*

In the comedy department, can you imagine American cinema without *Animal House, Ghostbusters,* or *Stripes*? Then thank Canada for Ivan Reitman. He's part of the Billion-Dollar Directors triumvirate (with Steven Spielberg and Robert Zemeckis) and he's generously given Americans lots to laugh about, with movies like *Dave, Kindergarten Cop* (in which he would direct future California governator Arnold Schwarzenegger, after the actor had been indoctrinated by Cameron in the *Terminator* films), and *Meatballs.* (However, with one meat-themed movie already in his repertoire, he was kind enough to allow an American a chance to direct the Canadian teen flick *Porky's.*)

YOU'VE BEEN CANUCKED

Many Americans laughed their way through *Strange Brew,* starring Canadians Dave Thomas and Rick Moranis— not realizing that Canada was purposely perpetuating the myth of the "beer-drinking hoser" to keep Americans complacent about its true power.

Other Canadians directing "American" classics include Arthur Hiller (*Love Story*), Norman Jewison (*The Thomas Crown Affair, Jesus Christ Superstar, Rollerball, Moonstruck*), David Cronenberg (*The Dead Zone, Naked Lunch, A History of Violence*), and Denys Arcand (*The Decline of the American Empire* and the Oscar-winning *The Barbarian Invasions*). And when it comes to, um, quality film, let us not forget the Lorne Michaels factor (see *SNL*, page 32); he produced *The Three Amigos, Wayne's World, Coneheads, Tommy Boy,* and *A Night at the Roxbury,* as well as the non-*SNL*-based hit *Mean Girls,* which launched the booze-and-media-circus spectacle of Lindsay Lohan mania.

AMERICA (?) THE BEAUTIFUL

Beyond dispatching Canadian operatives to found Hollywood's major studios and to direct, produce, and star in many of its biggest hits, Canada itself has frequently starred on screen. You know those glorious American film locations, those purple mountain majesties above the fruited plain? It's actually Canada, Canada, Canada. The breathtaking American West of *Unforgiven, Legends of the Fall,* and *Brokeback Mountain*? (Try Alberta.) *Chicago*? (Toronto.) *The Hotel New Hampshire*? (Quebec.) *Lake Placid*? (British Columbia.) *3000 Miles to Graceland*? (Vancouver.) *Aspen Extreme; Mystery, Alaska; Texas Rangers;* and *Rumble in the Bronx*? (British Columbia, Alberta, Alberta, and Ontario and B.C., respectively.) By cleverly luring film production north of the border through irresistible economic enticements, Canada ensures that any pride of place or visual recognition of

QUEBEC CITY, QUEBEC   CANADIAN ROCKIES, ALBERTA   VANCOUVE

America the beautiful is actually transposed upon the Homeland. It goes further still. Where does Santa live (in *Elf* and *The Santa Clause*)? Why, Vancouver and Ontario. What do Shanghai (*Shanghai Noon*), Tibet (*Seven Years in Tibet*), Russia (*The Russia House*), or even Mars (*Mission to Mars*) look like? They look like Canada. *The Scarlet Letter*? *American Gothic*? *Wild America*? Well, you get the picture.

YOU'VE BEEN CANUCKED

TV's *21 Jump Street*, set in LA. *MacGyver,* set in dangerous locations around the world. *Smallville,* set in Superman's Kansas hometown. *The X-Files,* set in the nation's capital (and other mysterious places). Four very different, very addictive shows over the past two decades, all set in very diverse places, but filmed in . . . Canada.

RITISH COLUMBIA

WHISTLER RESORT, BRITISH COLUMBIA

TORONTO, ONTARIO

CANADA'S SECRET WEAPON: HOTTIES

"They must be doing something right up there in Canada." —Hugh Hefner

On paper, Canada's major exports are agricultural products, natural gas, and lumber. In truth, though it may be cool up north, hotties are actually Canada's main gift to the world. Besides noteworthy Pamela Anderson (a former Labatt Beer girl born on Canada Day in 1967), Neve Campbell, and Kim Cattrall, here's a short list of fair Canadian lasses sent to colonize the dreams of untold Americans.

Rae Dawn Chong: The much-better-looking offspring of Canadian comedian Tommy Chong.

Elisha Cuthbert: Canadian Kiefer's divine daughter-in-distress on *24.*

Linda Evangelista: This cat-eyed supermodel has come a long way since winning Miss Teen Niagara in her native land.

Kimberly Conrad Hefner: The only gal to tame the Hef, this Playmate of the Year married the ultimate Playboy on—yep, Canada Day.

Margot Kidder: The former flame of Canadian PM Pierre Trudeau rocketed to fame as the headstrong and fetching Lois Lane in the first four *Superman* films.

Avril Lavigne: This hot young rocker gives a generation of skater boys another reason to veg out in front of MTV.

Carrie Leigh: Yet another Hef girlfriend and *Playboy* babe.

Evangeline Lilly: The hottest castaway on *Lost,* Lilly ranked No. 2 on *Maxim*'s Hot 100 Babe list.

YOU BE THE JUDGE

How Canadian is *Playboy,* an American institution (and red-blooded male distraction)? Playmate icons Pamela Anderson, Shannon Tweed, Dorothy Stratten, Carrie Leigh, and Kimberly Conrad are all Canadian, the latter of whom married Hugh Hefner on Canada Day, ending his thirty-year bachelor streak with a decade-long marriage. Interestingly, after nearly ten years of separation, they still haven't divorced—could it be that she's actually running the empire while he's out frolicking with the Girls Next Door?

Rachel McAdams: The star of *Mean Girls, Wedding Crashers,* and *The Notebook* was too classy to bare her bum with A-listers Scarlett Johansson and Keira Knightley on an infamous 2006 *Vanity Fair* cover (she's still Canadian, after all!).

Carrie-Ann Moss: Kicking ass in boots of shiny pleather in the *Matrix* trilogy, this Canadian costarred with semi-Canadian Keanu Reeves (who was born in Beirut but raised in Toronto).

Sandra Oh: The *Sideways* and *Grey's Anatomy* star was named one of *People* magazine's 50 Most Beautiful People.

Ellen Page: The pint-sized hottie from Halifax who broke through to stardom in *Juno*.

Dorothy Stratten: The former Playmate of the Year and lover of director Peter Bogdanovich suffered a tragic death, inspiring two movies and two hit songs by fellow Canadian Bryan Adams.

Shania Twain: The best-looking thing to happen to country music, Twain boasts the biggest-selling album of all time by a female artist (see page 65).

Shannon Tweed: Another former Playmate of the Year, Tweed cast her spell over multiple Kiss albums as Gene Simmons's main squeeze.

Estella Warren: The girl with the lips from Tim Burton's *Planet of the Apes* was No. 1 on *Maxim*'s Hot 100 Babe list; she credits synchronized swimming (invented in Canada!) for her rockin' bod.

AND GUYS TOO, EH?

Canada has also strategically deployed a dreamy fifth column of strapping male hotties to the States, from perennial heartthrobs Kiefer and Keanu to Brendan Fraser, Hayden Christensen, Ryan Gosling, and Ryan Reynolds— the latter of whom gallantly broke it off with Canadian fiancée Alanis Morrisette in order to continue being an object of lust for American girls (going on to grace *People* magazine's summer 2007 "Hottest Bachelors" list). Oh, and Halle Berry's baby daddy? Canadian hottie Gabriel Aubry!

WHAT YOU

HEAR

CANADA: TAKING CARE OF (THE MUSIC) BUSINESS

"Somehow, these four Canadians [wild cheering]— and one from Arkansas—defined America like no band before or since." —Tom Hanks on The Band, at the 2008 Grammy Awards.

Ah, music, the soundtrack to our lives. Think about how music affects you: all it takes is the right song to make you feel fired up or mellowed out, happy or sad, romantic or nostalgic. It is, in short, an open door to our emotional unconscious, and it should be no surprise that Canada has been orchestrating the very songs that make us sing our hearts out, tap our toes, or drive a little faster on our interstate highways. While hot Canadian artists top our charts and ace Canadian record producers mastermind hits that play our feelings like maestros, Canadian researchers have been quietly studying the effect all this has on us. Psychologists and neuroscientists at the University of Toronto, McGill University, and the Université de Montréal are studying the effects of music on the brain, working within an institute called the International Laboratory for Brain, Music and Sound Research (BRAMS)—perhaps to further hone their already effective sonic conquest of American minds. And so, just as we swoon at the magnificence of the American (Canadian) West on the silver screen, when we turn up the volume on our earbuds, we are all unknowingly humming, whistling, or singing Canada's tune.

YOU BE THE JUDGE

Did President Johnson discover the truth about Canada's musical influence on his constituents? Why else would he take the time to send personal letters praising radio stations that *didn't* play music by Canadian '60s icon and activist Buffy Sainte-Marie? (Luckily, his campaign didn't stop her from later winning an Oscar—and American moviegoers' hearts—for penning "Up Where We Belong," the uplifting tune from *An Officer and a Gentleman.*)

CAN'T GET YOU OUT OF MY HEAD

The most effective delivery system for Canada's subliminal sweet nothings is, of course, the catchiest of songs. The most insinuating examples of these are known as "earworms," upbeat melodies, riffs, or lyrics that get stuck in the brain and stay there, creating a sort of cognitive itch. Advertisers use them to insidious effect, and in the wrong hands (consider the Baha Men's "Who Let the Dogs Out?" or the theme to *Entertainment Tonight*), they can stun all other intelligent brain activity. But our Canadian masters would never harm us so. They want to use music to spread their own messages, sure, but they also want us to feel good *Canada Canada,* about ourselves *Canada Canada,* about our lives, *Canada Canada,* about . . .?

YOU BE THE JUDGE

Is Joni Mitchell's hit "Both Sides Now" actually about both sides of the forty-ninth parallel that ostensibly "divides" the United States and Canada? ("But now it's just another show/You leave 'em laughing when you go/And if you care, don't let them know/Don't give yourself away . . .") *Hmmm*?

Originally released across genres and even decades, bet you can hum every one of these catchy Canadian hits:

♪ "Constant Craving," k.d. lang

"Working for the Weekend," Loverboy ♪

♪ "Daydream Believer," Anne Murray (by way of the Monkees)

"Summer of '69," Bryan Adams ♪

♪ "Sunglasses at Night," Corey Hart

"Tom Sawyer," Rush ♪

♪ "Rockin' in the Free World," Neil Young

"Born to Be Wild," Steppenwolf ♪

♪ "Seasons in the Sun," Terry Jacks

"Safety Dance," Men Without Hats ♪

♪ "Takin' Care of Business," Bachman-Turner Overdrive

"She's Having My Baby," Paul Anka ♪

♪ "Ironic," Alanis Morrisette

"Building a Mystery," Sarah McLachlan ♪

♪ "One Week," Barenaked Ladies

"Mmm Mmm Mmm Mmm," The Crash Test Dummies ♪

♪ "Sundown," Gordon Lightfoot

"Auld Lang Syne," Guy Lombardo ♪

♪ "Girlfriend," Avril Lavigne

Humans have amazing auditory recognition and retention, with a few notes bringing a full song into our brains, and often, storing it there for quite some time. We might hear something in passing—say, a few notes of an old Loverboy tune, a catchy Shania Twain refrain, or even the *Facts of Life* theme song that we haven't heard in twenty years, and we find that not only can we hum along with ease, we can't get it out of our minds. And the sheer ubiquity of music today, on radio, popular TV shows, on our computers and portable players, means that we're incessantly exposed to the perfect medium for Canada's secret messages. When the time is right, the tune just seems to be . . . there. On AM, FM, satellite, and college radio; on Muzak while shopping or emptying your wallet in Vegas (see page 77), Canada "takes care of business" by quietly unleashing a song that furthers its cause—without anyone even realizing it.

The foundations for the plot were laid early—as early as 1889, with Canadian-born Alexander Graham Bell and Emile Berliner's invention of the gramophone. In its eventual technical refinements and popularization over the years, the gramophone would revolutionize music by conveniently allowing Americans to bring record players and music *into their own homes* in addition to the radio, a platform Canadians would also dominate. (The Canadian Broadcasting Corporation, which rules the Homeland's airwaves, still mandates that a specific quotient of Canadian music must be played on the radio every day by law—and this seems to be tacitly enforced south of the "border" as well.)

Soon, Canada was on a roll in the music biz. In the 1920s and '30s, when many American homes still didn't have record players, who sold more than 100 million albums in the U.S.? Why, Canadian Guy Lombardo. And thinking six moves ahead as would a chess grand master, Canadian Hugh Le Caine laid the groundwork for a time when synthpop and electronic music would seize the popular imagination, inventing the music synthesizer (and, arguably, making disco a possibility) back in 1945.

YOU'VE BEEN CANUCKED

Canadian bandleader Guy Lombardo's version of *Auld Lang Syne,* performed with The Royal Canadians, is still what Americans hear as the first song of the new year when the ball drops in Times Square. *Variety* once described Lombardo as "the only Canadian ever to create an American tradition." (Oh, if they only knew the truth . . .)

Canada quickly and shrewdly moved in to cover all types of music, to reach the maximum number of Americans: AM radio staples (Paul Anka, Anne Murray, Gordon Lightfoot), folk (Joni Mitchell, Buffy Sainte-Marie, Bruce Cockburn), eternally cool singer/songwriters (Neil Young, Robbie Robertson, Leonard Cohen), and current hot acts (Hot Hot Heat, Feist, Nelly Furtado). Why, Canada even takes care of classic rock (BTO, Rush, The Guess Who), '80s cheese (Loverboy, Bryan Adams, and—yes!—Corey Hart), and big-ticket Vegas acts (from Robert Goulet to Céline Dion). Their success inspired even more success. Canadian singer Rufus Wainwright, for example (son of Canadian folkster Loudon Wainwright III), was moved by Men Without Hats' breakthrough: "It was just the most glorious moment of everybody's lives to see someone from Montreal on MTV." Clearly, Canada's plan was working.

Face facts: when Canadian bands come on the dial, no matter what your taste, you simply can't resist. Which gives Canada plenty of opportunity to send its messages through speakers and earbuds nationwide.

YOU'VE BEEN CANUCKED

Canadian Alan Thicke is responsible for the TV theme songs Americans still hum, including those for *Diff'rent Strokes, Facts of Life* ("The facts of life are all about you"), and the original *Wheel of Fortune*.

Consider this:

🎵 Who sang the Oscar-winning theme song of the biggest movie of all time? A Canadian, Céline Dion.

🎵 Who has the best-selling album by a female artist ever? A Canadian, Shania Twain, for *Come On Over*—she edged out fellow Canuck Alanis Morisette, who held the honor until 2000 for *Jagged Little Pill.* (Oh, and who was the worldwide number-one best-selling female artist of 2007? Alanis's heir apparent Avril Lavigne.)

🎵 Who holds the record for the world's most successful rock single (and second-best-selling single ever, after "We Are the World")? A Canadian, Bryan Adams, for "(Everything I Do) I Do It for You." And "We Are the World"? That one happened to be engineered by Canadian Bob Rock and arranged for the Live-Aid concert finale by Canuck Paul Shaffer.

Even when the music seems, well, almost un-American, we love it all the same. Consider The Guess Who's 1970 No. 1 U.S. hit "American Woman" ("American woman, stay away from meeeeheee"), which criticized American "war machines and ghetto scenes." And it's hard to think of a more pointed statement than Joni Mitchell's "Big Yellow Taxi" ("They paved paradise, and put up a parking lot"), which would sting if we weren't so distracted by singing along. And do Americans really only want to be "working for the weekend," fueling the Canadian economy and living for the chance to race home and relax with six-packs of discounted Molson's and Labatt's, or a stiff shot of Canadian Club? Apparently, we do.

AMERICANA = CANADIANA

Canada has long been at the root of American roots music: Robbie Robertson and The Band, ranked by *Rolling Stone* as one of the 100 Greatest Artists of All Time, toured with Bob Dylan and influenced artists like Joan Baez, Johnny Cash, and Jerry Garcia, all of whom covered their tribute to rural Americana, "The Night They Drove Old Dixie Down." Seminal talents like Joni Mitchell, Buffy Sainte-Marie, Leonard Cohen, Bruce Cockburn, and Neil Young wrote the songs that the whole country swayed along to from the '60s on, from activist anthems to uplifting ballads, and they continue to influence countless American folk and rock acts to this day. Even the famed Man in Black, Johnny Cash, was shrewd enough to hire a Canadian manager and promoter, Saul Holiff, to guide his career through the '60s and '70s.

YOU BE THE JUDGE

Why would 2008 U.S. presidential candidate Hillary Clinton choose a Canadian tune—Céline Dion's "You and I"—as her official campaign song, if not as an attempt to secure the support of the true northern powerbrokers?

EH-MERICA THE BEAUTIFUL

Canada has really been influencing Americans through music from the beginning. Take a look at this:

EH-MERICA? → AMERICA THE BEAUTIFUL

CANADA IS ACTUALLY 350,000 SQ KM MORE SPACIOUS THAN THE U.S.

O beautiful, for spacious skies

WAVES = SHORELINE, WHICH CANADA HAS 10 TIMES MORE OF THAN THE U.S.

For amber waves of grain,

GRAIN = RAPESEED/ CANOLA: SEE PAGE 92

For purple mountain majesties

Above the fruited plain!

PURPLE MAJESTIES = ROYALTY: THREW THAT IN AS A FAVOR TO OLD PAL BRITAIN

McINTOSH APPLE, ANYONE? SEE PAGE 97

America! America!

God shed his grace on thee,

And crown thy good with brotherhood

CROWN = QUEEN

From sea to shining sea!

CANADA'S OFFICIAL MOTTO? A MARI USQUE AD MARE (FROM SEA TO SEA)

YOU DID IT
WHOSE ШAY?

Then there are those two "American" icons, both well known and beloved by the entire population: Johnny Carson and Frank Sinatra. One was the king of late-night TV, who routinely came into millions of homes for three decades. The other is one of the most famous American singers of all time, Ol' Blue Eyes. Their defining musical moments? *The Tonight Show* theme song set the tone for the evening and helped ease Carson into America's bedrooms and comfort zone. Frank Sinatra's best-known song is an anthem to self-expression and striking out on one's own that America holds so dear, "My Way." Interestingly, both were written by Canadian Paul Anka. (As Alanis would say, isn't it ironic?) And from the Rat Pack to the rug rats, "My Way" is now influencing an even younger generation on the sound track to the Oscar-winning, animated penguin kid flick, *Happy Feet.* But wait, there's more. What song did *Harry Potter* mega-author J.K. Rowling say would have been played at Dumbledore's funeral? Yep, that would be "My Way."

So, what Canadians are the kids of today listening to on their portable MP3 players?

cPod

Arcade Fire
Black Mountain
Broken Social Scene
The Dears
Feist
Godspeed You Black Emperor
Hot Hot Heat
Julie Doiron
Metric
Neko Case
Nelly Furtado
The New Pornographers
Peaches
Sloan
Stars
Tegan and Sara

EXHIBIT EH?

CANADIAN IDOL

American Idol is a television phenomenon in the U.S., reeling in number-one ratings week after week, hobbling American productivity in the workplace with watercooler gossip and keeping our citizens on speed dial, generating passionate phone-in voter turnouts our ailing political system should be so lucky to enjoy. In a perfect encapsulation of the power of

Canada's cultural operations to drive us to action—when the time comes—who are the millions of Americans unknowingly casting their ballots for? Canada.

Kelly Clarkson is the nation's first and arguably most successful American Idol. When she decided to ditch the packaged act and do a cooler album to express herself, she called it *Breakaway* (note the nod to Paul Anka's "My Way"); the eponymous first single off the album debuted in the Top Ten, going on to sell more than five million copies in the era of stealing/downloading songs for free. Who wrote it? No, not Anka this time, but another Canadian: Miss Avril Lavigne. (Winnipeg songwriter Chantal Kreviazuk also penned hits for the record.) But that's not all. *Idol* season two runner-up Clay Aiken, the unexpected tween heart-throb who commands an army of "Clay-mates" from coast to coast, is produced by Canadian Bob Rock. And hey, what song did *American Idol* play every single time another hopeful was voted off the show in its highly-rated fifth season? Why, "(You Had a) Bad Day" by Grammy-nominated B.C. singer Daniel Powter. The relentless exposure of this Canadian song poised it to become the best-selling digital single in the United States with 1.7 million downloads. (By the way, having a good day is season five fan favorite Kellie Pickler, who has been dating Nunavut-born hockey star Jordin Tootoo; he whisked her up to the remote Canadian territory to meet his family in 2007, marking her first trip to Canada. Don't be surprised if she comes back to Nashville singing a new tune . . .)

CANADA:
TURNING IT UP TO 11

Perhaps you're thinking, "Sure, I like Neil Young and the Arcade Fire, and OK, guilty, I was singing Loverboy in the shower this morning, but none of my other favorite music is *Canadian*." Well, read between the liner notes—not wanting to obviously hog the mic all the time, Canadian producers have been shaping the sound tracks of our lives, behind the scenes and soundboards, up and down the dial for decades.

Toronto-born Jack Richardson launched his career as a music mogul when he mortgaged his house to produce the star-making first album by The Guess Who (featuring the smash "These Eyes" and also the tellingly Canadian tune "Maple Fudge"); they later went on to become the first Canadian band to have a number-one hit in the U.S. with "American Woman." Richardson would go on to produce and executive produce albums by a constellation of 1970s "American" rock heroes such as Alice Cooper, Poco, Badfinger, and the Allman Brothers. He often worked with Canadian cohort Bob Ezrin, who was behind the console on Lou Reed's *Berlin,* multiple Kiss albums (including *Destroyer*), Peter Gabriel's first solo record, Pink Floyd's *The Wall* (on which he also contributed orchestral arrangements), as well as albums by the Jayhawks, The Darkness, Deftones, and Nine Inch Nails. Richardson's son, Garth, was behind Rage Against the Machine's first record, the Red Hot Chili Peppers' *Mother's Milk,* and albums by L7, the Melvins, the Jesus Lizard, Kittie, Atreyu, System of a Down, and Canadian crossover group Nickelback.

Ever play air guitar to "Enter Sandman," "Dude Looks Like a Lady," or "Dr. Feelgood," or sing your heart out to "You Give Love a Bad Name" or "If I Could Turn Back Time"? Then you've enjoyed the Canadian stylings of Ontario-born producer and engineer Bob Rock, who helped create these and other monster hits for Metallica, Aerosmith, Mötley Crüe, Bon Jovi, Cher, and dozens of other artists (including Homeland favorite The Tragically Hip).

YOU BE THE JUDGE

Was Canada—which boasts rockin' tunes, a predilection for plaid, and a close proximity to the Pacific Northwest—responsible for unleashing the grunge music trend on the U.S.?

ET TU, U2?

Canadian musician and sonic craftsman Daniel Lanois produced or coproduced such seminal albums as Bob Dylan's *Oh Mercy* and *Time Out of Mind,* Emmylou Harris's *Wrecking Ball*, Peter Gabriel's *So* and *Us*, Willie Nelson's *Teatro,* Dashboard Confessional's *Dusk and Summer*, and U2's *Unforgettable Fire, The Joshua Tree, Achtung Baby*, and *All That You Can't Leave Behind.* (And the Edge's trademark soaring guitar sound? It's thanks in large part to Canadian Michael Brook, who invented the "infinite guitar," outfitted with a feedback transducer to produce nondecaying sustain of any note—you can hear it most clearly on the opening of "With or Without You" from *The Joshua Tree).* Lanois also composed music for the notably "American" films *Sling Blade* and *The Last of the Mohicans.*

YOU BE THE JUDGE

When Matt Stone and Trey Parker made *South Park: Bigger, Longer, and Uncut,* did their song "Blame Canada" seek to expose Canada's controlling influence over every aspect of American life? It was a close call, but luckily for Canada, Americans took the song as a farce, and the secret remained safe.

YOU'VE BEEN CANUCKED

Even Superfreak Rick James had a Canadian connection. Relocating to Toronto to escape the U.S. Naval Reserves, he formed a band with an unknown Neil Young and future Steppenwolf member Nick St. Nicholas; their first release as the Mynah Birds was with the Canadian arm of Columbia Records.

But the true mastermind of "American" modern popular music, whose reach extends across rock, soul, pop, jazz, hip hop, R&B, movie sound tracks, and beyond, is Canadian musician-composer-writer-producer David Foster. Scoring a No. 1 Canadian and American hit in 1973 for the song "Wildflower" with his short-lived band Skylark, he would also perform as a keyboardist with the likes of John Lennon, Diana Ross, Rod Stewart, George Harrison, and Barbra Streisand. In his multihyphenate capacity, he's embodied the Canadian goal of covering every genre on the American dial by working with (ready?): Clay Aiken, the Bee Gees, Deborah Blando, Andrea Bocelli, Brandy, Toni Braxton, Garth Brooks, Michael Bublé, Mariah Carey, Peter Cetera, Chicago, Natalie Cole, the Corrs, Céline Dion, Destiny's Child, Earth, Wind & Fire, Josh Groban, Ronnie Hawkins, Faith Hill, Julio Iglesias, Michael Jackson, Al Jarreau, Chaka Khan, Gordon Lightfoot, Kenny Loggins, Madonna, Richard Marx, Katharine McPhee, Luis Miguel, Anne Murray, 'N Sync, Olivia Newton-John, Dolly Parton,

YOU'VE BEEN CANUCKED

Even American icon Elvis Presley wasn't immune to Canadian influence; he was so swayed by Bachman-Turner Overdrive that he adopted the motto "takin' care of business in a flash" as an homage to their song, and gave his entourage necklaces with the letters TCB and a lightning bolt. The Big E also gave a nod to Canadian songwriters and singers by recording songs by Gordon Lightfoot, Buffy Sainte-Marie, Gene MacLellan (including "Snowbird," a huge hit for Canadian songbird Anne Murray), and his own take on Paul Anka's "My Way."

Lisa Marie Presley, Kenny Rogers, and Vanessa Williams. He's won fourteen Grammys (including three for producer of the year) and been nominated forty-two times, including Grammy and Academy Award nominations for Whitney Houston's "I Have Nothing" from *The Bodyguard* sound track. He also produced the eternally catchy *Footloose* sound track and, oh yeah, in order to cover the sports buffs, he composed the "Winter Games" theme song for the 1988 Calgary Olympics, as well as "The Power of the Dream," the official song of the 1996 Summer Olympics (sung by Céline Dion). "Winter Games" is also played at the popular fountain show at both Sea World and the Bellagio resort in Las Vegas. And speaking of Vegas . . .

JACKPOT

OPERATION VEGAS

PAYS OFF

What happens in Vegas may stay in Vegas, but the great bundles of U.S. greenbacks spent there are funneled up north through the Canadian music and entertainment operations firmly established in this Sin City playground. It's all part of the master plan, a brilliant moneymaking endeavor in which Canada doesn't have to risk anything on a roll of the dice. What could be easier, safer, or more lucrative than to set up strangely irresistible big-name Canadian acts, charge upward of $300 per ticket, and convert the loot into loonies? Though it's difficult to confirm, sources indicate that the money goes to fund the ongoing development of Canadian entertainers to be sent across the "border" to ensure future revenue and continuing musical indoctrination into the Canadian way of life. (You should see who they're grooming for Caesar's Palace in 2020—you might as well book tickets now, and they ain't gonna be cheap!)

SPECIAL AGENT DION **Céline Dion**, Canada's biggest little moneymaker, was trained, primed, and packaged for sale to the U.S. from the get-go. Her latest coup? For four solid years, Céline performed five nights a week to sold-out crowds in a custom-built stadium at Caesar's Palace, where she personally raked in more than $100 million (plus a percentage of the profits) from Céline-ophile Americans, who also dropped dough in an exclusively Céline gift shop. The diminutive French-Canadian songbird has also scaled the walls of that American institution called Disney, winning an Academy Award and a Grammy for the theme song to 1991's *Beauty and the Beast.* The hit—produced by Canadian David Foster—went to No. 1 in the U.S. only a year after her Anglophone debut, making her a star and an icon to countless knee-high American girls. Then she scored big-time with "My Heart Will Go On," the Oscar-winning theme song of the highest-grossing movie of all time, *Titanic* (directed by fellow Canuck James Cameron, see page 48). Meanwhile, she's steadily accumulated record sales in excess of $175 million and is the best-selling female artist not just in America, but in the world.

SPECIAL AGENT GOULET The late Vegas resident and icon **Robert Goulet**, the only son of French-Canadian parents, kicked off his career up north with fellow Canuck William Shatner on the Canadian version of *Howdy Doody*. When not handily selling out shows to the older set in Vegas, the singer-actor graced an American Emerald Nuts campaign, which showed him cheekily hindering U.S. productivity with a wink and a smile.

SPECIAL AGENT LITTLE Another Vegas-based operative, Canadian **Rich Little** has raked in the dough for decades by (ironically) doing softly satirical impressions of U.S. presidents; he also hosted the 2007 White House Corre-spondents' Dinner, a handy one-stop shopping locale to check up and report back on the state of U.S. political and media operations.

SPECIAL AGENTS CIRQUE DU SOLEIL The Quebec-based avant-garde circus and entertainment empire first toured the States in 1987 and has been raking in the francs in Vegas since the early '90s with five different shows on the Strip, tightrope-walking their way into the hearts of more than 33 million spectators in over 130 cities worldwide.

YOU BE THE JUDGE

Did Canada ask Alanis to contribute to the dumbing down of America with her song "Ironic" (which features a variety of sing-along situations that are, ironically, *not*)?

MADE IN CANADA

Not only does Canada control how we entertain ourselves, it has also woven itself tightly into the social, economic, and physical fabric of our daily lives.

Trade between the United States and Canada is staggering in volume—clocking in at around $1.5 billion *a day.* Canada and its southern satellite province have been each other's largest export trading partners since the 1940s. By the U.S. State Department's own estimates, 65 percent of U.S. exports are bound for Canada and contribute millions of jobs to the American economy (Canada is the main export market for thirty-nine of the fifty states). Meanwhile, nearly 80 percent of Canada's exports are headed for the U.S. market (but *shhh*, no "Made in Canada" labels). The State Department also figures that about three hundred thousand people flit to and fro across the "border" daily.

YOU'VE BEEN CANUCKED

Canadian-American economist John Kenneth Galbraith has been one of the key figures in shaping American social and economic policies. His influence extends from developing socioeconomic policies and writing speeches for Presidents Roosevelt, Truman, Kennedy, and Johnson, to helping conceive of Johnson's Great Society program against poverty and racial injustice (which included Medicare and Medicaid). In more than forty books, thousands of articles, and over twenty-five years of teaching at Harvard, he ensured a vast legacy for his policies and principles, which included critiques of unregulated capitalism and excessive private wealth accumulated at the expense of public needs. He also coined the term "conventional wisdom," a concept Canada's been expertly spinning ever since.

This constant Canadian influence permeates all aspects of our lives, in ways we've never even considered. For example, in addition to inventing the lightbulb, the choco-late bar (*mmmm,* Canada-licious) and time as we know it (see page 99), the first commercial jetliner to fly in North America was designed by Canadian James Floyd, and the electric streetcar, another linchpin of American transport, was introduced by Canadian John Joseph Wright back in 1883. (And if your luggage made it to your destination, thank John Mitchell Lyons, who invented the separable baggage check tag way back in 1882.)

YOU'VE BEEN CANUCKED

Canadian Alfred Fuller of Fuller Brushes pioneered the practice of door-to-door solicitation—an annoying but effective technique to reach all members of society, even those without cable or a PDA. Next time your doorbell rings during dinner, remember, it's Canada calling!

Canada has also dispatched operatives in a variety of key industries that have shaped America and helped ensure that it's a good asset for Canada's portfolio. Canadian Herbert Henry Dow, founder of Dow Chemical, still the largest producer of plastics in the world, ushered in a new consumer era that relied on the convenience of Tupperware, Ziploc bags, and Saran Wrap ("one word: plastics"). James Lewis Kraft, a grocery clerk from Ontario, founded Kraft Foods with his Canadian brothers to keep our pantries full. Today the company sells more cheese than any company in the world, and is the largest branded food and beverage product company in North America (and second largest in the world), home to everyday brand staples like Oreo, Miracle Whip, Jell-O, Oscar Mayer, Planters Peanuts, and Maxwell House. And when America needed a fresh look, Canadian Frank Gehry was sent down to help shape modern architecture—and became the only architect familiar enough to the U.S. masses to be featured on *The Simpsons.*

All this in addition to inventing myriad life-improving (and sometimes life-saving) products—everything from household items to medical necessities to booze—and sprinkling them across every level of our society for us to find and use (and sometimes take credit for), like bonus gadgets in the video game of normal American life. And while Americans blindly rely on these Canadian items day in and day out, Canada has been quietly encouraging a feel-good mythology of "American" ingenuity, capitalism, and know-how. American schoolchildren even believe that the telephone was invented in America, and that Superman is an American hero! If they only knew. Look around and you'll see Canada everywhere. Everywhere!

YOU'VE BEEN CANUCKED

North America's first department store was Canada's Hudson's Bay Company, which sold your great-great-grandmother her first wool blanket—at a nice markup. (You can thank Canada the next time you stop by your local Macy's, Sears, or Target.)

EXHIBIT EH?

INVENTED IN CANADA:
COMMUNICATION

Alexander Graham Bell, whom you've probably heard of, finally admitted that he came up with the whole telephone thing in Canada, saying, "It was conceived in Brantford (Ontario) in 1874 and born in Boston in 1875." Interestingly, Bell was living in Canada the year he devised, tested, and first demonstrated the phone, yet he quickly moved to the United States the following year when it was time to secure the patent—ensuring that America could take the glory and no one would be the wiser. As predicted, Americans loved the phone, and Canada suddenly had an easy way to hear everything they had to say without leaving the comfort of the home country. The phone is just one of many eaves-dropping, er, communication devices invented by Canada, including the walkie-talkie, the CB radio (keep on truckin', America!), the cordless phone, the telephone pager, and the ubiquitous BlackBerry, a handy way to monitor the text messages, Web visits, phone calls, and cute little emoticons of more than eight million Americans daily.

YOU'VE BEEN CANUCKED

It took Canadian physicist George S.K. Wong to kindly point out that the accepted figure for the speed of sound had been incorrect for decades, and was fast by about half a mile per hour.

And Canadian surveillance goes way beyond just creating the means of communication and monitoring our daily chatter. Edmonton-born media theorist and "patron saint" of *Wired* magazine Marshal McLuhan described the influential cognitive effects of media in shaping thought and interactions ("the medium is the message"), though he carefully avoided pointing fingers at who has been pulling the strings. Sure, Canada has found clever ways of controlling media *content* in a multitude of ways, but beyond that, it has found equally ingenious methods of controlling the physical and broadcast media themselves. Canadians invented newsprint made from wood pulp, effectively creating a way to circulate information and boost Canadian lumber sales simultaneously. And throughout communication history, there's Canada helpfully crafting creations like the undersea telegraph cable, short-wave radio, the first audio radio broadcast, the television system, the Java computer programming language, and the TV V-Chip, to control what we hear and see all day long. And really, is it such a stretch to believe that the country that controls the BlackBerry is the country that rules the world?

POWER = *POWER*

But wait, there's more! Canada also commands the raw energy that runs many of these communication necessities. Oil? It may surprise you that Canada, not Saudi Arabia, is the number one exporter of oil to the United States. Ditto for petroleum, hydroelectricity, and natural gas. Even canuck-devised kerosene, a cleaner burning, more efficient, and whale-protecting oil, is still in use as fuel today. But beyond raw power, Canada also invented clever ways to deliver this energy—and extend its influence. Canadian Lewis Frederick Urry invented both the lithium and the long-lasting alkaline battery for Eveready, inspiring the new brand name "Energizer." The original prototype now shares a room at the Smithsonian with another unsung Canadian invention, the lightbulb, which was invented in 1874 by medical student Henry Woodward and his buddy Matthew Evans. (The invention was too flashy to hold on to; the pair would sell the American and the Canadian patent a year later to Thomas Edison for a mere $5,000 U.S.)

YOU BE THE JUDGE

Among the many possible origins of the phrase "the real McCoy" is the likelihood that it refers to Canadian inventor Elijah McCoy . . . and perhaps also identifies Canada as the one who's *really* in charge?

CANADA,
WE HAVE LIFTOFF

When Canada needs to evaluate the really big picture, it monitors things from space. The Canadian Space Agency runs its own active space program, which remains fairly hush-hush to avoid scrutiny of what it's actually looking at. As in other industries, Canada deflects the limelight to the United States, graciously waiting until America had a satellite in space before sending up its own *Alouette 1* in 1962. (It's interesting to note that while *Alouette 1* was built and funded entirely by Canada, it was launched from Vandenberg Air Force Base in California . . . an ideal United States surveillance point.) The launch of *Anik A-1* in 1972, also from the U.S., made Canada the first country in the world to have its own domestic geostationary communication satellite network—all the better to watch us with.

In addition to its own mysterious forays into space, Canada has managed to watch over and influence America's as well. Canada contributed to the success of the American space program from the first blast-off with the invention of the **antigravity suit** (or G-suit)—originally called the Franks Flying Suit, after University of Toronto scientist Wilbur R. Franks—sending Canadian technology up with military pilots, astronauts, and cosmonauts since 1940. More recently, eight Canadian astronauts have been on board to keep a watchful eye on a dozen NASA manned space missions since 1984. And let's not forget the extraordinary robotic arms invented in Canada, the **Canadarm** on the Space Shuttle and **Canadarm2** on the International Space Station, both allowing Canada to literally get its (mechanical) hands on whatever is happening in the stratosphere.

INVENTED IN CANADA:
HEALTH

Canada is wise enough to protect its investment in the United States and the American people by keeping them healthy and strong—all the better to do Canada's bidding. In Canada, where life expectancy is a full three years longer than in the United States, citizens have enjoyed government-funded national health care for nearly fifty years. While Americans continue to resist the concept, at least they've learned to sneak up north to get cheaper prescriptions, which Canada strongly encourages. Canada's good works extend from the establishment of the first hospital in North America (in 1644, in Montreal, by Jeanne Mance) to its discovery of stem cells (by Canadian cellular biologist Ernest McCulloch, with James Till). Healthy Americans mean productive minions! To further this goal, Canada has sent down some key health-related inventions to help its Americans thrive (and its own economy to prosper).

CANOLA OIL The United States is the biggest customer for this healthier cooking oil made from rapeseed, invented and produced exclusively in Canada; the word *canola* is derived from "Canadian oil, low acid."

CPR DUMMY When Americans need resuscitation, it's Canada who gives them mouth-to-mouth.

DENTAL MIRROR Think of it this way—at every checkup, Canada is looking down your throat.

ELECTRIC PROSTHETIC HAND Canada, giving Americans a helping hand since 1971.

ELECTRIC WHEELCHAIR Canadian George Johnn Klein invented the first electric wheelchair for quadriplegics as well as the first microsurgical staple gun.

ELECTRON MICROSCOPE It took a big, big country to help Americans see things that are very, very tiny.

FOGHORN This helpful safety device has kept countless ships from crashing—but not Canadian Gordon Lightfoot from scoring a stateside hit with "The Wreck of the Edmund Fitzgerald."

HEART PACEMAKER Winnipeg-born Dr. John Hopps made sure American hearts beat for Canada.

INSULIN Isolated by Canada, yes. Invented? The jury's still out on that. Either way, it comes in handy when digesting all that delicious Canadian maple sugar.

And let's not forget the **ABDOMINIZER** If another round of Labatt's isn't your idea of a "six-pack," then America owes a big debt to this infomercial exercise darling, invented by Canadian Dennis Colonello in 1984.

INVENTED IN CANADA:
EVERYDAY NECESSITIES

Think of it as product placement on a massive, nationwide scale. Canada has cleverly planted its own inventions everywhere Americans turn—and not only that, it has made sure these products are indispensable to daily life. Although most of us don't know it, Canada has invented the household items we can't live without, from the zipper to the electric stove, from the garbage bag to the beer case. Add in the ginger ale in your fridge, the Nickelback CD in your stereo, and the probability that the car parked in your garage (or many of its parts) were made in Canadian factories, and chances are at this very moment your household is up to 70 percent Canadian! Ask yourself this: At what point do we reach the tipping point and *become Canadians ourselves*?

CANADIAN BACON   Just imagine a "Hawaiian" pizza or a delicious eggs benny brunch without this salty Canadian staple.

CHOCOLATE BAR   Americans would only get gum out of vending machines if not for New Brunswick chocolatiers

Arthur Ganong and George Ensor, who invented the chocolate bar in 1910.

ELECTRIC CAR HEATER Ever driven in Saskatchewan in December? Thomas Ahearn invented the first electric car heater in 1890.

ELECTRIC COOKING RANGE Canadian Thomas Ahearn also invented this ubiquitous household appliance in 1882 and was the first person to cook a meal on it. Without him, Americans might still be heating up their Kraft Dinner over a campfire.

FROZEN FISH FILLETS Like its time-saving counterpart, instant mashed potatoes, this Canadian invention has freed up countless cumulative hours for quality time around the TV with our families.

GARBAGE BAG Canada's contribution to American cleanliness since 1950.

YOU BE THE JUDGE

Is Tim Hortons poised to be the next Starbucks? The ubiquitous Canadian food-and-coffee chain named for a former hockey great—which holds 62 percent of the Canadian coffee market, compared to Starbucks' measly 7 percent—has begun seeping into the United States with more than three hundred outlets. If you start craving an addictive bite-size ball of hot dough called a "Timbit," blame Canada.

GREEN INK The green on your greenbacks is thanks to a currency ink invented by Canadian Thomas Sterry Hunt in 1862.

JOLLY JUMPER Thank Canada and Olivia Poole for this parenting essential, which allows Americans to keep their hands free while baby bounces.

KRAFT DINNER What would American kids, college students, and bachelors do for fuel without handy mac & cheese in a box, invented by Canadian entrepreneur James Lewis Kraft, the genius first to patent processed cheese? (As founder and president of Kraft Foods for nearly fifty years, he also bequeathed cheesy goodness in the form of Kraft Singles, Velveeta, and Cheez Whiz to American homes.)

LAWN SPRINKLER Without Canada's help, your kids would have to run through boring old air in your backyard. The inventor, Elijah McCoy, also gave us the folding ironing board and an automatic lubricating system to help trains and machinery run faster.

LIGHTBULB Contrary to popular (American) belief, the first electric lightbulb was invented and patented in Toronto in 1874 by Henry Woodward and Matthew Evans, who sold a share of the patent (and all of the limelight) to Thomas Edison.

MARQUIS WHEAT Dubbed "the wheat that won the West," this cold-resistant wheat gave Canada its famed amber waves of grain in 1908; thirty years later, Thomas

Carroll invented the self-propelled combine harvester to bring it to market.

McINTOSH APPLE Every McIntosh apple, widely thought to be the superior apple for applesauce, pies, cider, and snacking, has a direct lineage to a single tree discovered by John McIntosh in Ontario in 1811. The eponymous American computer didn't fall far from the same tree (see below).

WHICH CAME FIRST, THE McINTOSH APPLE OR THE APPLE MACINTOSH?

Why the fruit, of course, grown, discovered, and named in Canada in 1811. Computer scientist Jef Raskin named the Apple Macintosh computer after the delicious Canadian apple in the 1980s—but alas, he adopted a common misspelling often seen in American grocery stores. Due to the continuing popularity of Macintosh computers, the misspelling lives on . . . and Americans everywhere live their iLives on computers sporting a Canadian-born apple as its moniker with a built-in, standard feature American typo. This elicits knowing, tolerant chuckles up north.

ODOMETER Canadian Samuel McKeen invented the first car odometer in 1854, helping to monitor exactly how far Americans are going.

YOU'VE BEEN CANUCKED

You may not know it by name, but Canadian snack treat *poutine*—a hearty concoction of cheese and gravy over fries—is the predecessor to many American munchies that involve goo-covered starch, from chili cheese fries to mini-mart nachos.

PABLUM Invented by Canadian pediatricians in 1930, this instant infant cereal was the original "breakfast of champions"—fast, healthful, and revolutionary.

PAINT ROLLER Invented by Canadian Norman Breakey in 1940, this invention has saved millions of Americans from unsightly brush strokes on their rumpus room walls.

PLEXIGLAS Poly (methyl methacrylate) was invented by Canadian William Chalmers in 1931; the shatter-free glass alternative has a staggering array of uses including aquariums, mod furniture, airplane windows, motorcycle helmets, contact lenses, and, of course, the spectator zone at hockey rinks.

POLYPUMP LIQUID DISPENSER Canadian Harold Humphrey made pumpable liquid hand soap possible in 1972.

SNOWBLOWER Natch.

SNOWMOBILE Ditto.

SNOWPLOW Snow more . . . it's too much!

SQUARE-HEAD ("ROBERTSON") SCREW AND SCREWDRIVER
Thanks to Canada, Americans can finally stop trying to put a square peg in a round hole.

STANDARD TIME Canadian Sir Sandford Fleming instituted a twenty-four-hour international clock based on the world globe meridian of Greenwich—making it much easier to accurately track the time of Americans' every move.

ZIPPER Canada's not *all* business—after inventing the lightbulb, Canucks improved and manufactured America's earliest zippers for those times when the lights are off.

SUPERMAN, THE GREATEST *CANADIAN* HERO

Superman has been our iconic national hero since the 1930s, inspiring young and old in comics, radio serials, television, and film. Kansas farm boy, big-city reporter, Man of Steel . . . and the creation of Canuck artist Joe Shuster (with American writer Jerry Siegel). Sent from the planet Krypton by way of Toronto, Superman lifted spirits during the Depression and helped instill "American" (Canadian) values at the dawn of FDR's New Deal, such as defending the powerless and serving as a bulletproof exemplar for "truth, justice, and the American way." This Canadian creation not only established the aspirational superhero genre, but also launched a brilliantly influential new media outlet in the process: the American comic book. Thanks to Superman, comics became an invaluable way to influence scads of even the youngest Americans, who faithfully followed their secretly Canadian hero's exploits as he helped shape their values at a formative age. (Later, Canadian cutie Margot Kidder would play his girlfriend Lois Lane in the first run of *Superman* films—as well as serving as half a power couple with former Canadian PM Pierre Trudeau—and British Columbia would stand in for Kansas on the small-screen series *Smallville.*)

Superman would also later enjoy a run as illustrated by popular comics artist and Canadian double-agent John Byrne (born in England, moved to Canada at age eight). In addition to making his mark on the Man of Steel and the Fantastic Four, Byrne would also illustrate a myth-making series called *The Uncanny X-Men,* featuring Canadian superhero Wolverine and introducing the first all-Canuck superhero team, Alpha Flight. The distinctly Canadian Spandex squad included the Guardian (sporting maple leaf tights), Aurora, North Star, Sasquatch, an aboriginal Canadian hero called Shaman, and Snowbird (shout out to Anne Murray!). Meanwhile, fellow Canadian Todd McFarlane—cartoonist, comic book writer, artist, toy manufacturer/designer, and media entrepreneur—became a superstar by reinvigorating the Spider-Man franchise, then launched the antihero Spawn for a new generation of American comic book readers. His toy empire, like the rest of Canada's media kingdom, spans the American pop cultural spectrum, including comic heroes and villains, rock idols such as Kiss, kiddie favorites like the Grinch, and edgier fare.

THIS ROUND'S ON *CANADA*

Clearly, Americans love to drink—almost as much as Canadians. And since the days of Prohibition, when Canada provided delicious contraband liquor to the dry United States, Canada has not been above using booze to manipulate us when necessary—either to enhance the American mood or to keep us buzzed and contentedly incurious about the true state of affairs. Ignorance never tasted so good. Cheers!

BEER Canadian beer—like Molson Canadian, Labatt Blue, Alexander Keith's, and Kokanee—isn't really stronger, it just mysteriously tastes better than the big American brews.

CANADIAN BLENDED WHISKY Classics include Crown Royal, Canadian Club, and Seagram's; Canada also made sure to send down the perfect mixer by inventing Canada Dry Ginger Ale.

THE CAESAR Only a very bold country would mix vodka and clams. The cocktail, also known as the Bloody Caesar, was invented in 1969 by Canadian hero Walter Chell, who crushed fresh clams into tomato juice and added plenty of vodka. Americans can now take the easy route by buying Clamato off the shelf.

ICE WINE Strong, sweet, cold wine from Canadian grapes that are stronger, sweeter, and colder than Napa's.

YOU'VE BEEN CANUCKED

Besides "rum-running" Canadian whisky into the States, Canada took advantage of America's experiment in Prohibition to launch a lucrative ginger ale business. The Canadian-invented soft drink—cleverly launched in the States the year before Prohibition—became both a substitute for booze and *the* favored mixer for bathtub gin. (In case you want to try this at home, an average bathtub filled with gin would make 2,560 highballs when combined with 1,280 bottles of icy cold Canada Dry Ginger Ale.)

RED EYE Also known as a Calgary red eye, this is Canadian beer mixed with tomato juice. Add an egg if you want. Brunch is served.

SCREECH If you haven't heard of this lethally strong rum, the official drink of Newfoundland, it's because it renders the average American unconscious.

YUKON JACK At the bar, a "double jack" is a combination of Canada's Yukon Jack and America's Jack Daniel's (needless to say, the Yukon Jack is on top and is a much larger pour).

YOU BE THE JUDGE

Would Americans drink as much beer as efficiently as we do without Canadian Steve Pasjack's 1957 invention of a beer case that had a built-in, tuck-away handle?

EXHIBIT EH?

WHAT YOU

THE *REAL* HOME TEAM

Okay, by now you are probably a bit freaked out by how much control Canada has over the United States—through Hollywood, frozen fish, Avril Lavigne, and all. It might feel like there's nowhere to run, and nowhere to hide—except perhaps in the sweet, simple escapism of good old American sports. Perhaps you figure you can turn off the music, dim all the lightbulbs, and ignore the telephone, blocking out all those things you now know to be Canadian to focus solely on the joy of a big game. Hey, even if you have to follow those beloved sports by watching them on TV, listening to them on the radio, or reading about them in newsprint (all of which were invented in Canada), at least Canada isn't the boss of the United States when it comes to actually playing the games themselves.

Or is it?

YOU'VE BEEN CANUCKED

Can't imagine watching your favorite games without instant replays? Thank George Retzlaff at the Canadian Broadcasting Corporation, who produced the first in-game replays in 1955 as part of Hockey Night in Canada, giving sports nuts everywhere a second chance to see what really happened.

Before you go high-fivin' your pals over America's domination of the sports world, you should know the whole truth: Canada has actually had a hand in the development of most U.S. sports. Yes, even if you are somehow unaffected by all of Canada's other attempts to control and shape your life (you hate ginger ale, don't care for Neil Young, and refuse to live your life according to standard time), if you're playing sports at all, you're playing for Team Canada.

When you think about it, it's no wonder Canada covers this territory as well; sports are the perfect distraction mechanism for the United States. Run up and down a basketball court for forty-eight minutes and you're too tired to stage a coup. And if, like most Americans, you follow sports in the media, cheer on your "fantasy" teams, bet in office pools, or tirelessly rehash the games with friends and family, Canadians can truly take over. It seems like there are always playoffs, tournaments, pennant races, March Madness, or an overtime upset to redirect attention on a national scale for weeks at a time, whisking away any burgeoning suspicion of Canada's deeper motives. ("Say, did you ever notice that it seems like Canada has an awful lot of influence over . . . oh hey, the game's on!") In the vicarious euphoria of post-game glory or the agony of defeat, no one remembers what they were piecing together from the shadowy suspicions beginning to take shape. So, while it's true that Canada didn't invent the jockstrap, you could say that they have you by yours.

EXHIBIT EH?

HOCKEY

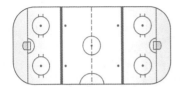 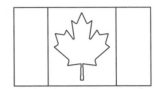

It's a given that Canada's pleasantly cold climate would lend itself to the development of hockey. Yes, Canadians invented this hallowed sport, and with Canadian operatives like Wayne Gretzky in L.A., Gordie Howe in Detroit, Bobby Orr in Boston, Mario Lemieux in Pittsburgh, Joe Sakic in Denver, Mark Messier in New York (we can't go on—it's embarrassing), Canada has had its agents skating all over America. And as long as there are rinks, it always will—if you freeze it, they will come. (The added benefit of the game's increasing popularity in the United States—thanks to these northern superstars—is its availability to all the displaced Canadian spies who have to live in America; having good hockey to watch down here is clearly part of their relocation package.)

YOU'VE BEEN CANUCKED

What's the oldest trophy competed for by professional athletes in North America? Hockey's Stanley Cup, originated by Lord Stanley, Governor General of Canada, in 1892.

BASKETBALL

This one seems unimpeachably American. Basketball conjures images of kids hitting the hoops on a sweltering blacktop, dreaming of a shot at NBA fame; nights spent shooting baskets in the driveway with your old man; and games of HORSE with some college buddies over cold beer. Well, enjoy your bastardized game of "Duck on a Rock" any way you choose. Canadian James Naismith, basketball's inventor and early custodian, would be proud of how it's caught on—and how it's changed very little since he nailed up a couple of peach baskets and published a list of rules back in 1891. Canada even opened the first YMCA in North America, so we'd all have a place to practice after school!

Although Canada has mostly let Americans have the glory in this sport, it does keep its hand in by occasionally offering up players like two-time NBA MVP Steve Nash (known as the Canadian Kid).

And what about the brilliant distraction ploy of March Madness? It's a fitting moniker: Americans are whipped into a mind-altering frenzy during the annual NCAA men's college basketball tournament, known as the Big Dance— where sixty-four games played in twenty days add up to nearly $4 billion in lost wages and productivity as fans are irresistibly drawn to the tube. Just what is Canada up to while everyone is conveniently fixated in a basketball trance for three weeks? Spring cleaning? Cooking the books before tax time? Only our masters up north know for sure, and they're not telling. Swish! It's another slam dunk for Canada.

"AMERICAN" FOOTBALL

OK, so you know that everywhere else in the world, the term "football" actually means soccer or rugby, right? Canada didn't want to tell us back then, mostly because we looked so happy running around holding on to the ball, thinking we had our own sport at last. Anyhow, to ensure that we wouldn't give ourselves concussions and damage Canada's American investment, Naismith stepped in here, too, and introduced helmets to U.S. football—since no Americans seemed to be coming up with the idea. And just to set the story straight, you probably ought to know that the first actual game of this new "American football" was played in Canada, between Harvard and Mr. N's alma mater, McGill University in Montreal, in 1874—a full year before it was played on American soil. Touchdown, Canada!

YOU'VE BEEN CANUCKED

What do the Washington Redskins (NFL), Los Angeles Lakers (NBA), and Los Angeles Kings (NHL) have in common? Canada, of course! This cross-sport trifecta was owned by Canadian entrepreneur Jack Kent Cooke, who also built the landmark Forum in Inglewood, California. (Oh, and in 1980 he added one more piece of Americana to his portfolio, purchasing the Chrysler Building.)

BASEBALL

Our national pastime is—you've probably resigned yourself to this by now—as Canadian as an apple pie baked with McIntoshes. If you're making a pilgrimage to Cooperstown's Baseball Hall of Fame, you might want to drive a little farther north to the tiny Canadian town of Beachville, just outside of London, Ontario. Alex Cartwright and Abner Doubleday may have been quiet on the subject, but the game held so dear to Americans is recognized by many as first played here, in Canada. Ouch—that hurts almost as much as catching a line drive without a glove. Would it help to know that the in-depth baseball resource and media company "Baseball America" was also started in Canada? Didn't think so.

YOU'VE BEEN CANUCKED

Tough Toronto-bred baseball player Arthur Irwin didn't want to miss a game after breaking two fingers, so he cleverly doctored up a driving glove—and Americans with perfectly good hands are still using his fielders' glove to help them succeed in this "American pastime."

CANADA'S A GOOD SPORT

If these big-money, big-dream sports don't capture your fancy, Canada has kindly provided a whole portfolio of other sporting activities on which you can focus your time and attention:

CURLING Most Americans laugh at this slow-paced "darts on ice" enterprise that Canucks continue to dominate with brooms and matching sweaters. But if global warming and *The Day After Tomorrow* have taught us anything, it's that the next ice age is coming, and soon—and our clever Canadian masters will already know how to run on ice. Good luck getting that last can of Pringles from the 7-Eleven.

YOU BE THE JUDGE

Is Canada the master of sports at sea as well as on land? Not only was the hydrofoil boat invented in Nova Scotia by Alexander Graham Bell and Canadian Casey Baldwin, the famed Canadian fishing schooner *Bluenose* defeated Gloucester, Massachusetts-based *Elsie* for the International Fishermen's Trophy in 1921, holding on to the prized cup for seventeen more years.

YOU'VE BEEN CANUCKED

Among the many American sports teams to use Canadian rockers Bachman-Turner Overdrive's "Taking Care of Business" during sporting events, the New York Mets played the song after victories during the 2006 season, and their division rival Atlanta Braves used the song during their run of fourteen consecutive division titles.

FIVE-PIN BOWLING A truly Canadian sport invented by T. E. Ryan of Toronto in 1909, this is another example of Canadians developing a simple game of knocking things over into one of tight precision and execution—plus, five fewer pins and a smaller ball means more energy to lift beers.

LACROSSE If there's an American out there who thinks he's too tough for basketball or football, Canada invented the roughest of all outdoor sports to keep the show-offs occupied.

SYNCHRONIZED SWIMMING Okay, so it's not goose-stepping, but if you dive into the pool and are tempted to start twirling, remember it was Canada who invented the moves. Swim, rummy!

TABLE HOCKEY It's a given that Canadians would find a way to get you to play hockey without ice. Many an unassuming college student has been taken for some beers and brainwashing over a rousing game at Canada's table.

FOR THE LOVE OF THE
(CANADIAN) GAME

Even if you turn off all outside media for the night—including TV sports—and gather your family around the coffee table for a good old-fashioned board game, Canada is still manipulating your every move. America's favorite (and multimillion-selling) board games—including Trivial Pursuit, Yahtzee, Balderdash, Scruples, and Pictionary—were all invented by Canadians. Win or lose, it's Canada that always earns the high score.

But even while it controls our every move, Canada's true intentions are still aimed at improving us. As with our favorite sports, these games instill a sense of fair play and good sportsmanship, and teach us skills that make us better able to fulfill Canada's needs. Yahtzee hones math acumen. Balderdash improves our vocabularies. Pictionary develops left-brain skills. And Scruples? It educates players about moral dilemmas and appropriate choices. So perhaps through these games—as well as game show tests of knowledge like Alex Trebek's *Jeopardy*—Canada is educating us to be better, smarter, and more thoughtful neighbors to them and to each other. (Case in point: Yahtzee, originally called "The Yacht Game" by its wealthy Canadian inventors, promoted itself to the U.S. market by promising "The game that makes THINKING fun!")

By now, you are most likely shocked, stunned, over-whelmed . . . simply in awe of the sheer genius of Canada and the scope of their dominion. And you may find your-self pining for the time when you were unenlightened, blindly believing the propaganda that the Homeland has been spoon-feeding you. But now that your eyes have been opened, it's time to face facts: Canada is the boss of you. And when you've had some time to think about it, you'll realize that it's not so bad. You can openly wear plaid. You can say "beaver" proudly, without giggling. You can finally revel in your secret love of curling. Americans get to live comfortably, happily even, in the shadow of a ruling country of funny, kind, beer-loving, toque-wearing demigods. Not so bad, eh? So, why fight it? Kick back, pop open a Blue, flip on the hockey game, and repeat after us:

It's good to be Canadian.

ABOUT THE AUTHORS

Kerry Colburn, an "American," and **Rob Sorensen**, a Canadian, are the authors of *So, You Want to Be Canadian,* also published by Chronicle Books. They live conveniently close to the 49th parallel in Seattle, with their two dual-citizen/double-agent daughters, Piper and Molly.

Once again, the authors thank Steve Mockus, Sara Gillingham, and the entire ever-so-talented gang at Chronicle Books (Crown's on us), as well as all our readers on both sides of the "border" who responded so well to our first book that it inspired us to write another. A special shout-out to all the 'nucks (especially shuck, metal, eck, shew, cody, vegas, spute, nev, fall, trio, baz, and chili) and all the other Canadians who have made such an impact on us, the United States, and the world proper—including Warner Bros. et al, for kicking things off, Lorne Michaels for bringing it home, and "Wild" Bill Shatner for keeping it real.